ACKNOWLEDGEMENTS

Without the help and cooperation of many people, the research for and writing of this dissertation could never have been completed. Sincere appreciation is expressed to all the following persons for their invaluable help in this project:

Dr. Robert O. Stripling, my chairperson, who gave freely of his time and support while inspiring high levels of graduate performance throughout the formulation and completion of this entire project.

Dr. Jordan B. Ray and Dr. James Wattenbarger, who gave their valuable assistance and encouragement throughout this project.

Dr. Benjamin Barger, who was there when I needed him.

Norman L. Hull, my husband, without whose love, commitment and efforts this project would not have been accomplished.

Freda and Leo Bernstein, my parents, who inspired my perseverance while providing much mechanical assistance.

Rebecca and Andrew Hull, my children, who gave me the future orientation needed to complete this project.

iii

TABLE OF CONTENTS

LIST OF TABLES

Abstract of Dissertation Presented to the
Graduate Council of the University of Florida in Partial
Fulfillment of the Requirements for the
Degree of Doctor of Philosophy

COUNSELORS' PERCEPTIONS OF SEX ROLE STEREOTYPES

By

Miriam Bernstein Hull

December 1979

Chairman: Dr. Robert O. Stripling
Major Department: Counselor Education

· The purpose of this study was to examine urban
community college counselors' perceptions of males,
females, and adults without regard to sex. The main
objective was to learn if male and female counselors
had different perceptions of males and females as compared to their perceptions of adults. Another objective
was to learn if there was any correlation between counselors' age and their perceptions of males, females,
and adults.

The subjects were 149 urban community college
counselors from seven southeastern states. A community
college was considered urban if it was located in a
Standard Metropolitan Statistical Area, as defined by
the U.S. Bureau of the Census. Each college was asked
to provide a list of counselors who had at least a
master's degree and who spent at least 50% of their

time in face-to-face contact with students or with other college personnel concerning students. In the 24 colleges that agreed to participate, 184 counselors met the criteria. Of these 184 counselors, there was a total of 87 male counselors and 62 female counselors whose data were usable (80.9% of the counselors who met the specified criteria).

The counselors were asked to complete one of the three forms (male, female, or adult) of the Sex Role Questionnaire produced by Rosenkrantz, Vogel, Bee, Broverman, and Broverman in 1968, and a cover sheet which included a request for demographic data. The Sex Role Questionnaire is composed of 36 bipolar items, each describing a characteristic attribute of an individual. The items are classified as to which pole is judged more socially desirable. A high score indicates greater social desirability.

Based on previous research, it was expected that male counselors would perceive males and adults as being similar and females as being different. These expectations were not supported. Using a completely randomized analysis of variance, the data indicated that there was no significant difference in the perceptions of males, females, and adults. Male and female counselors perceived males, females, and adults in similar terms. However, it was found that male counselors had slightly greater expectations for males than female counselors did, and female counselors had greater expectations for adults than did male counselors. There was no difference between male and female counselors in their expectations of females.

There was no significant correlation ($p < .05$) between the ages of the counselors and their perceptions of sex role stereotypes. When an additional analysis was performed, computing the correlation between the years since the counselors' last degree and their perceptions of sex role stereotypes, no significant correlation ($p < .05$) was found. It was concluded that sex role steroetypes are not as fixed as earlier studies had indicated, at least as perceived by community college counselors in seven southeastern states.

CHAPTER I
INTRODUCTION

During the 1960's and the 1970's the interrelated issues of sexism and attitudes toward women have become central concerns of American society, and have posed anew the philosophical question of woman's role within the fabric of society. Sexist attitudes and sex role stereotyping tend to limit female potential and restrict males into immutable roles. Cultural norms may deter an individual from pursuing a goal which would serve best both his own and society's interests. Cultural lag may explain to some extent why societies cling to outmoded beliefs and attitudes about both men and women. For counselors within an educational community these outdated common beliefs may be reinforced by theories which define the counselor's role as helping an individual adjust to the cultural norm. The expressed desires of educators have been to emphasize the individual and to help each student achieve his/her potential; however, until sexism and stereotyping are removed this may not be possible.

Purpose of the Study

Because sex role stereotyping is an educational problem demanding attention, the purpose of this study was to provide empirical data about the sex role perceptions of urban community college counselors. The study surveyed urban community college counselors because it was believed that when changes in societal perceptions occur, they would be first manifested in urban areas. The population for this study was drawn from the southeastern states of Alabama, Georgia, Florida, Mississippi, North Carolina, South Carolina and Tennessee.

Sex role stereotypes are highly consensual norms and beliefs about the differing characteristics of men and women. Evidence of the existence of such sex role stereotypes is abundantly present in the literature (Broverman, Broverman, Clarkson, Rosenkrantz, and Vogel, 1970).

Broverman et al. (1970) reported that mental health clinicians described both males and females very stereotypically (males/aggressive/females/submissive). More importantly, the traits ascribed to a nonsex specified adult were less likely to be applied to a woman than to a man; in fact, the male description was virtually identical to that of the sex unspecified adult while the female description differed significantly. Furthermore, the researchers compared the American

societal perpetuation of the female sex role stereotypes
with the "pre-civil rights ideal Negro" stereotypes of a
conforming, obedient, submissive black who is well
adjusted to his society. The former ideal Negro stereotype is, of course, no longer valid; and analogously, it
is probably true that the stereotypes perceived by the
subjects in the 1970 Broverman study are no longer completely valid.

There has been much publicity and concern about
the changing role of women. In the 1970's the attention
given to sex role stereotypes ascribed to women has been
greater than at any other time in history. Cancian
(1975) investigated publicity on topics related to the
women's movement by counting the proportion of listings
devoted to "women" in the New York Times Index and the
Reader's Guide to Periodical Literature between 1965 and
1974. The number of listings was constant from 1965 to
1968, but there was a significant increase between 1969
and 1970. In fact, during 1969 and 1970, the listings
devoted to women constituted a full 2% of the total, the
largest percentage of topics ever written about women.
It was believed reasonable to assume that counselors
have experienced the influence of the women's movement.
Current research was needed to ascertain whether there
had been any change in sex role stereotypes of both men
and women.

At all educational levels counselors are the
official resource persons for students seeking assistance concerning personal, educational, and career decisions. Counselors have the potential to influence, not
only students but also the counseling profession,
instructors and administrators (Verheyden-Hilliard, 1977).
Counselors' perceptions about men and women are a significant factor in the counseling process (Oliver, 1975).
By learning the perceptions that counselors have about
sex role stereotypes, there should be more knowledge
of the expectations that counselors bring to the counseling situation (Pietrofesa & Schlossberg, 1970).

There has been a dearth of research reported in the
literature on the community college counselor. With
growth of college enrollment, the community college has
been the avenue many women have chosen for both entry
and re-entry into the world of work. Within community
colleges, programs and courses for, and about, women
have been organized. Indeed, community college counselors themselves may have enrolled in courses concerning the psychology of women. Therefore, there is a professional responsibility to engage in research on the
contemporary beliefs and sex role perceptions of community college counselors.

The age of the community college counselor may be
related to the counselor's perception of sex role

stereotypes. There is a tendency for older people to adhere to more traditional beliefs, and older women customarily support traditional roles for women. Ryder (1965) reported that when new cohorts of women enter a population (i.e., a given profession) they can effect an attitude change in all members of that population. It would appear that the sex role perceptions of both young counselors (sex unspecified) and women counselors (both older and younger) are becoming liberalized to a greater extent than those of older women and male counselors. In addition to investigating whether there is a difference in male and female counselors' perceptions of males and females and the relationship of each to the adult stereotype, this research was designed to determine whether there existed any correlation between the age of counselors and their perceptions of sex role stereotypes.

Statement of the Problem

Male stereotypic characteristics traditionally have had a higher societal value than female stereotypic characteristics (Lynn, 1962; Rosenkrantz et al., 1968). As indicated above, mental health clinicians perceived the male in almost identical terms to those in which they perceived the sex unspecified adult (Broverman, et al., 1970); and their perception of the female was significantly different from that of either the male or adult. Previous studies have indicated that both male and female counselors had the same stereotypic perceptions of adults, males and females. However, most of the studies concerned with sex role stereotypes were conducted prior to the women's movement. Because that movement has had so much influence on educated women, it was believed that women counselors in urban community colleges would now make fewer distinctions based upon sex role stereotypes. It was also believed that male counselors in the same institutions probably would perceive adult and male stereotypes as similar while the female stereotype would be perceived as different from either adult or male stereotypes.

Because younger people have had greater exposure to the women's movement and younger counselors may have had courses, workshops and access to literature on women not originally available to older counselors (Stevens, 1971), it was further predicted that younger counselors would have a less traditional perception of the female and would perceive the adult, the male and female very similarly. More specifically, the questions answered by the research were:

1. Do male and female counselors practicing in urban community colleges have different perceptions of

males and females, as compared to their perceptions of adults?

2. Is there a correlation ($p < .05$) between counselors' ages and their perceptions of males, females and adults?

Hypotheses

I. There will be no difference ($p < .05$) in the means among groups receiving male, female and adult instructions on the Sex Role Questionnaire.

II. There will be no interaction effect ($p < .05$) between the sex of the counselors and the type of instruction (male, female or adult) on the Sex Role Questionnaire.

III. There will be no positive correlation ($p < .05$) between the ages of the counselors and their perceptions of the male, as scored on the Sex Role Questionnaire.

IV. There will be no positive correlation ($p < .05$) between the ages of the counselors and their perceptions of the female, as scored on the Sex Role Questionnaire.

Definition of Terms

Throughout this study, certain terms are used that have specialized or limited meanings. The following should help to clarify some of these terms:

Stereotype--A fixed standard or concept of attributes of a class of persons or social values. Once formed, stereotyped impressions are extremely resistent to change (Krech, Crutchfield & Livson, 1970).

Role--The kind of behavior expected of an individual because of his place within social arrangements. Any one person fulfills or adopts numerous roles on varied occasions (Hilgard, Atkinson & Atkinson, 1975).

Sex Role--The behavioral patterns, attitudes and characteristics of members of one sex (Cox, 1973).

Traditional Female--A woman who discontinues her career commitments to become a full time wife and mother (O'Connell, 1976).

Nontraditional Female--A woman who does not interrupt her paid career commitments to become a wife and mother (O'Connell, 1976).

Neotraditional Female--A woman who interrupts paid employment for child rearing and later resumes career commitments (O'Connell, 1976).

Adult--A nonsex specified physically mature person. For the purposes of this study, adult is operationally defined as a nonsex specified person whose characteristics conform to the majority of the counselors' perceptions of an adult.

CHAPTER II
REVIEW OF THE LITERATURE

Studies which have explored the problem of sex role stereotyping have approached the area from three general perspectives. Because many counselors define their role as assisting people to be integrated into their society, one group of studies has investigated the significance of the acquisition of the appropriate sex role standards to which a person should conform to be considered well adjusted in our society.

Second, given counselors' paramount consideration for the individuality of the client in a therapeutic situation and the client's perception of self, researchers have been concerned with the interrelation between sex roles and self-concept. The third set of studies focuses on counselors' sex role perceptions of their clients in a counseling situation, what sex role standards counselors consider socially desirable, and how such sex role perceptions have affected counselors' professional contact with clients.

Sex Role Acquisition and Societal Adjustment

Many counselors perceive their role as that of helping people to become integrated into society.

Societies hold tenaciously to antiquated beliefs and attitudes. Thus, while conditions of life today have changed, many of the cultural attitudes remain basically unchanged. This is especially true with regard to sex role stereotypes.

Most sex role research has focused on the women. The masculine stereotype, however, is equally real and defined (Wong, Davey & Conroe, 1976; Kirkman, 1977). The need for approval and affirmation often has locked men into role conformity out of fear that expression of individuality would bring ridicule and stigmatization (Harrison, 1978). Men have been denied the right to develop their dependent, emotional selves (Stevens, 1974). Boys are assigned many conflicting roles and are expected always to be in control (Nelson & Segrist, 1973).

> Men in America are taught a set of rules about the meaning of masculinity, almost from the moment of their birth, which has the effect of splitting their egos off from most of their emotions . . . . A real man must prove his masculinity. . . . Masculinity must be constantly tested: by the ability to make the first string Little League team; by the number of girls and the amount of money he can "make. . . ." Unless the individual's achievements meet the fixed criteria laid down by these rules, he is not a real man, he is a eunuch. (Stevens, 1974, p. 16)

More than for a woman, it seems important for a man to understand his sex role since it appears that "high self-esteem in males is a function of early success in meeting cultural standards of masculine behavior" and is "contingent on continued success in meeting cultural standards of masculine achievement" (Hollender, 1972, p. 344).

A male may have a difficult time in developing the sex role he needs for self-esteem (Miller, 1973). A man must accomplish something to earn or prove his masculinity. It is not ascribed by society to all persons who are bio- logically males. Males, more than females, are punished for acting in ways typical of the opposite sex. Girls may be tomboys, but boys may not be "sissies" (Tibbetts, 1977). Men are not as free as women to express their feelings of fear, hurt, and grief. Men learn that they must always cope and never admit defeat. Because men have fewer societally acceptable alternatives, they com- mit more suicides and, if single, are more likely to be mentally ill (Sexton, 1970).

Sex role distinctions are fostered early in the developmental process. The implicit assumption is that acquiring an appropriate sex role is a desirable pro- cess. Brown (1957) reported that the acquisition by the child of normal sex role behavior was fundamental to total personality development and adjustment. He reported that girls at each age level were more variable in their sex role preferences and urged that girls be encouraged to develop their femininity early.

However, Baruch (1974) found that the children who were least likely to gain in intelligence over a fixed time period were those who measured highest in the trait of femininity in psychological tests; that is, the brighter and the more feminine the female was as a youngster, the smaller the gain in intelligence as she grew older. On the other hand, the brighter the boy in intelligence the greater the gain in intelligence. Adjustment and self-esteem were negatively related to being feminine. Competence was a male-valued trait and the girls who perceived themselves as competent did not consider themselves as socially valued. Even when women have been found to be equal to men, in intelligence, they have not contributed equally to society (Farmer, 1976).

Because psychologists have accepted societally imposed sex roles as essential to personal adjustment, psychopathologists have considered disturbances in adjustment attributable to inadequate gender identity. Counselors and clients alike have tended to focus upon the conditions and processes which facilitate success-ful internalization of appropriate sex role standards. This approach may not, however, be conducive to the development of the full capabilities of the client.

Psychologists generally have accepted the traditional sex role ideology dividing the vast range of human possibility into two mutually exclusive spheres (Harrison, 1978). Bem (1972) postulated two reasons why psychologists have produced a literature that portrays the world as composed of feminine females, masculine males and sex reversed deviants. She first hypothesized that psychologists' sex ideology was predicated upon an "adjustment" theory of mental health which emphasized that it was desirable for children and adults to conform to society's sex role standards. Bem challenged this adjustment theory, suggesting that "the evidence reviewed so far suggests that a high level of sex appropriate behavior does not necessarily facilitate a person's general psychological or social adjustment" (p. 7). She also found no correlation between appropriate sex role behavior and intelligence.

Bem then researched an aspect of psychological "traits." Trait theory assumes that there are consistencies in an individual's behavior that are cross-situational. However, she reasoned that inconsistency is the norm and it is the phenomenon of consistency which must be explained. Using the Bem Sex Role Inventory, she found that masculine and androgenous subjects did not differ from one another in amount of conformity, and they conformed on fewer traits than

feminine subjects. Bem, therefore, called for a re-
examination of the basic psychological theories which
promote the concept of sex typing and adjustment.

Clearly the acquisition of a sex role by an individual both identifies and limits that individual. The
literature suggests that the sex role which society has
used to define the role of women has limited women to a
far greater degree than now appears justifiable and has
hindered a woman's individual development by denigrating,
in the name of adjustment, her capacity for achievement
within society.

Sex Role and Self-Concept

According to Rogers' self-theory, accurate perceptions and the subsequent integration of social expectations with personal values are essential to adaptive
development. He states that conflicts between personal
goals and social norms are likely to occur least for
flexible individuals who can find a variety of ways to
integrate personal values and social demands (Rogers,
1951). If sex roles do not correspond with what people
think of themselves, with what they think others want
them to be, and with what they ideally would like to be,
psychological conflict results.

There are many concepts and perceptions that
people believe about themselves and the opposite sex which

affect their behavior in society. Women choose to be in a subordinate position, but that choice may not be a free, intelligent, educated one (Tibbetts, 1975). Women fear not being feminine; yet having traditional feminine traits is not accompanied by high self-esteem (Baruch, 1974). When each is asked to describe his own sex, men emphasize desirable, positive characteristics while women tend to criticize themselves and express unfavorable traits. Because women do not respect themselves, a woman who breaks out of her traditional role may lose rather than gain the respect of her fellow females (Hacker, 1957).

This loss of respect is separate from the marginal position in which the nontraditional female finds herself when she tries to enter a traditionally male territory. Some men are threatened by this rivalry and will use economic, legal and/or ideological weapons to eliminate and reduce the competition and conflict (Rosen & Jerdee, 1975). The woman, feeling this tension within herself, and in her relations with the people around her, both male and female, may retreat easily to her traditionally feminine role which serves much like a womb--warm and comfortable, but restricting.

Rose (1951) found that men are self-determined while women determine themselves by reference to men. To study whether women have a less adequate expectation

of themselves, he chose subjects from similar socioec-
onomic backgrounds. In such a group Rose found that
men were more independent in their choosing of marriage,
number of children and out-of-home activities. Although
the women polled expected to spend larger amounts of
time at home and rear larger families, their answers
were very dependent on choices to be made by the men in
their lives. The women who chose a career along with
homemaking, when asked to estimate how many hours a day
they spend in various activities, discovered that their
proposed day exceeded the 24 hours allotted to them.
This gave credence to the career women's feeling that
they were unable to accomplish all they hoped. Komisar
(1970) concurred with Rose that men have a greater sense
of self than women; and that while marriage is one aspect
of a male's life, it is usually the major focus of the
female's life.

Vavrick and Jurick (1971) reported a high correlation between a man's attitude toward himself and his
attitude toward others. Male upper classmen and graduate students responded to Thematic Apperception Test
cards and were scored for self-concept and attitude
toward their wives' characters. The females could be
viewed as whole persons, as being somewhat stereotyped,
or as sex objects. Ninety-four percent of the males

scoring high in self-concept perceived females as whole
persons or being only slightly stereotyped, while 85 of
those with poor self-images thought of females as pri-
marily sex objects. None of the subjects scoring low in
self-concept thought of females as whole persons. Thus,
the male who views women as sex objects may also suffer
from a low self-image.

The number of conflicts that women experience
involving nonhome roles tends to decrease if the women
perceive the male's stereotype of femininity to be
patient, supportive and unemotional (Gordon & Hall,
1974). Women who work sense a greater difference between
their self-image and that of feminine women. In the male
dominated environment outside the home women perceive
that males have a more stereotypic standard of femininity.
Therefore, a woman's public self is more likely to conform to the stereotype than her private self.
Athanassiades (1977) reported differences among the self-
concept, public self and the perceptions of the female
stereotype. He suggested that the female stereotype is
not internalized, but acts as an external constraint on
the behavior of females. The counselor must be aware
of this societal constraint in a counseling situation.
The objectives of counseling should be to modify modes
of thinking to help the female make choices consistent

with personally established values rather than choices that simply conform to society (Dellas & Gaier, 1975).

A woman's sense of identity is a reflection of her role as wife and mother. O'Connell (1976) studied 87 middle class college educated women who were classified either traditional, neotraditional or nontraditional (see definitions). The neotraditional and traditional women perceived their identity as comparatively stronger and in more personal terms at the stage when their children were in school than at earlier stages in the life cycle. As child bearing duties diminish, the focus of their identity became more internal and personal. The nontraditional women perceived their identity as comparatively strong at all stages of the life cycle.

Competition by women with males is considered taboo in our society. Hauts and Entwisle (1968) suggested that for achievement motivation to be manifested in performance, women must perceive their goals acceptable within the female role. With ability held constant Hauts and Entwisle found that if masculine competitive behavior was deemed appropriate for the female role, there was a positive relationship between achievement attitude and school grades. Hacker (1957) found that men accepted women on the greatest level of intimacy, wifehood, but not at the level as associate or partner; and the excelling of the male over the female in college was due to the female's acceptance of the inferior role assigned to her. The more likely a girl was to accept the traditional female role, the more likely she would enter into noncompetitive disciplines. The female mathematics/science major tended to be more career oriented than the liberal arts major. The career-oriented female had a greater need for independence while her desire for submissiveness was less evident (Cross, 1968; Astin, 1968).

What is implied by this phenomenon is that there is a personality variable that differentiates career versus home-oriented females. The working women of today have intrinsic rather than extrinsic motivations to work. Personality factors are as important as financial factors (Wolfe, 1969; Ohlsen, 1968). This is not to imply that women need not work for money and survival.

Seltzer (1975) reported that students were considering more diverse roles. She hypothesized that freshmen women would be more utilitarian and accepting of change and innovation in role orientation than upper class women because they had less anxiety about not being married and also had experienced more exposure to the feminist movement. She found that the freshmen

were only slightly less traditional. She suggested
that more alternatives needed to be presented to women
early in their schooling and that counselors should
present these alternatives positively.

Nontraditional females were more likely to have
received counseling in their education (Ginzberg, 1966;
Astin, 1968; Ginzberg & Yohalem, 1966). Properly timed
awareness of alternatives can be decisive in securing
students' maximum use of abilities without great waste
of human and material resources. Males need to be
encouraged to assume more helping roles while women
need to assume more leadership positions and better use
of their mechanical and technical aptitudes (Rieder,
1978). Students recognize the need for counseling,
expressing sentiments much like this female student who
dropped out from a school before taking her oral examination for a doctorate:

> It occurs to me that some kind of counseling
> on the campus would perhaps have shown me
> what I couldn't perceive myself. My graduate
> adviser . . . certainly tried to be helpful.
> But he was one of the very people whose every
> concern was making me feel more and more
> idiotic and embarrassed and making it all the
> harder for me to pass the orals . . . . Had
> I known of any disinterested person on cam-
> pus whose function it was to hear and advise
> on such matters, I should have seen him
> early. As it was, I ended simply by running
> away. (Ginzberg, 1966, p. 43)

Women of all levels of skill need encouragement to develop this wide range of aptitudes. They must know the outlets available to them.

Sex role confusion is not only a problem for females. Both men and women adjust their lives toward what they think is desirable to the opposite sex. Counselors are sought to facilitate this adjustment process. However, to achieve such adjustment, one must know what the opposite sex desires.

Steinmann and Fox (1966) and Steinmann, Fox and Forkas (1968) conducted two studies, one on male and female perceptions of the female sex role and the other on male and female perceptions of the male sex role. The first study included 837 women and 423 men, in an age range from late teens through seventies and with the majority age under 40. They used the Inventory of Feminine Values which contains 34 statements, each of which expresses a particular value or value judgement related to a woman's activities and satisfaction. Half of the items defined a self-achieving woman as one who considers her own satisfactions as equally important with those of her husband and family and wished opportunities to realize her latent talents. The other items defined a family-oriented woman whose satisfactions came second after husband and family and who considered her family responsibilities as taking precedence over any potential personal occupational activity.

The females responded to three forms of the inventory: how they themselves felt, how their ideal woman felt, and how they thought men would want a woman to respond. Men responded to these items as they thought their ideal woman would respond.

The responses were analyzed by the percentage of same and different modal responses. The results indicated that most women delineated a self-concept relatively balanced between strivings and self-realization and vicarious fulfillment through other-achieving or intra-family strivings. The ideal woman, described by the female subjects, was more active and achieved more than the subjects themselves; but at the same time she maintained her family and other indicia of the traditional female role. The women's perceptions of man's ideal woman was a woman significantly accepting more of a subordinated role in both personal development and the familial structure.

The ideal woman delineated by men was a woman relatively balanced and not significantly different from the woman's own self-perceptions. Thus, there was a discrepancy between what women thought men wanted and what the men did, in fact, desire.

The second study (Steinmann, Fox & Forkas, 1968) focused on the male. Using the Inventory of Male Values, the respondents could delineate a family-oriented man who sought no status or position outside the family, or a self-achieving man who considered his own satisfaction of prime importance. The subjects were 441 males and 663 females with a wide variety of backgrounds. The men answered three forms: self-perception, their ideal man, and what they thought a woman would answer in terms of her ideal man. Women responded first in terms of their ideal man, and, second, as to how they thought a man would answer the inventory.

Male self-perception was relatively balanced to the two extremes of the inventory. Their ideal man was more active and self-assertive than they judged themselves. The male's perceptions of the woman's ideal man was more family-oriented than either male's self-perceptions of his ideal man. The woman's ideal man was more self-achieving than man's self-image but almost identical to the ideal man that men described for themselves. Women described their ideal man as active and self-assertive, but assumed that other men were more self-achieving than their ideal man.

The two studies show that while both sexes had the same ideal image for each sex, neither sex had a perception of how the other felt. The researchers concluded that sex role confusion exists for both men and women. Communication is the necessary link and counselors need to be aware of their biases and attitudes in order to facilitate communications between the sexes.

Rosenkrantz, Vogel, Bee, Broverman and Broverman (1968) used a 122-item Sex Role Questionnaire to study the relationship of self-concept to differentially valued sex role stereotypes in male and female college students. The 36-item Sex Role Questionnaire used in this research is a shorter form of the same questionnaire developed for the Rosenkrantz et al. (1968) study. Because of the questionnaire's significance in later research and in the present study, the process by which it was developed merits more extensive discussion.

The Sex Role Questionnaire was developed because the researchers believed that many of the traditional masculinity/femininity scales, such as the California Psychological Inventory, were based on traditional notions of sex-appropriate behavior that were no longer relevant. The researchers' concerns were related to the traits and behaviors currently assigned to men and women. Approximately 100 men and women enrolled in three undergraduate psychology classes were asked to list all the characteristics, behaviors and attributes on which they thought men and women differed. In the responses, 122 items had appeared at least twice, and these 122 items were selected for inclusion into the questionnaire. The items spanned a wide range of content, including interpersonal sensitivity, emotionality, aggressiveness, dependence, independence, maturity, intelligence, activity level and gregariousness.

Rather than having subjects select from a list of those traits which characterize men and those traits which characterize women, as was the method of previous studies (Fernberger, 1948; Sherriffs & Jarrett, 1953; Sherriffs & McKee, 1957), Rosenkrantz et al. (1968) conceptualized sex role stereotypes according to the degree to which men and women were perceived to possess any one particular trait. Therefore, the 122 items were put in a bipolar form with the two poles separated by 60 points.

Both male and female subjects were given the Sex Role Questionnaire with instructions to indicate the extent to which each item characterized an adult man (masculinity response) and the adult woman (femininity response) and themselves (self-response). The order of presentation of masculinity and femininity instructions was reversed for approximately half the subjects. However, the self-instructions were always given last so

as to obtain self-descriptions within a masculinity/
femininity context.

The concept of sex role stereotype implies extensive agreement among people as to the characteristic differences between men and women. Those items on which at
least 75% agreement existed between the subjects of each
sex (80 college women and 74 college men) as to which
pole was more descriptive of the average man than the
average woman and vice versa were termed stereotypic.
Forty-one items met this criterion. Correlated t tests
were computed between the average masculinity and the
average femininity response to each of the items; on
each the difference was significant (p > .001) in both
the samples of men and women.

Forty-eight of the remaining items had differences
in each sample between the average masculinity response
and the average femininity response which were significant beyond the .05 level of confidence, but the agreement as to the direction of difference was less than 75%.
These were termed differentiating items. The remaining
33 were termed nondifferentiating items.

The Sex Role Questionnaire was later reduced to 82
items. It consisted of 76 items taken from the original
form plus six new items. Approximately 1000 subjects,
ages ranging from 17 to 54 and from varied religious,
educational and social backgrounds, filled out the

original questionnaire, using these standard instruc-

tions:

> We would like to know something about
> what people expect other people to be like.
> Imagine that you are going to meet someone
> for the first time, and the only thing that
> you know in advance is that he is an adult
> male. What sort of things would you expect?
> For example, what would you expect about his
> liking or disliking of the color of red? On
> each scale put a slash and the letter "M"
> above the slash according to what you think
> the adult male is like.

The questionnaire has three sets of instructions:

Male (M), Female (F) and Adult (A). The (F) and (A)

instructions simply substitute the words "woman" or

"adult" for the word "male." The 82-item form contained

those stereotypic concepts on which the agreement among

the subjects that a pole reflects masculine rather than

feminine behavior or vice versa differed from chance at

the .02 level of confidence. Consensuality for the six

new items was found in smaller samples.

In 1974, the Sex Role Questionnaire was reduced to

36 items, 24 male-valued (MV) (competency) items and 12

female-valued (FV) (warmth, expressiveness) items. This

was the same ratio of competency to warmth items as was

in the 82-item form. The item selection was based on

responses from 1051 women and 763 men. All subjects

were paid volunteers who filled out the 82-item form.

They varied in marital status, education (seventh grade

to doctoral level), age (17 to 54), religion and employment status.

The percent of subjects who agreed that men had more of a particular trait than women or vice versa was computed for each of the 82 items. All items on which there were less than 60% agreement in either the male or female sample were discarded. Correlated t tests between the ratings of men and the ratings of women for each item were computed separately for the male and female samples. Items on which the t did not reach the 5% level of confidence were discarded. Twelve FV items and 35 MV items met the criterion of 60% agreement in both the sample of men and the sample of women. To maintain the same MV to FV ratio of the 82-item form, the MV items were reduced to 24 by eliminating items with lower levels of agreement.

Correlations between the 82-item form and the 36-item form were computed for a variety of samples. These correlations were significant (p < .001) and very high, ranging from a low of .901 to .950 for the MV responses and from .852 to .936, for the FV responses. Thus, the 36-item version of the Sex Role Questionnaire seems to measure the same dimension as the long form of that instrument.

Rosenkrantz et al. (1968) hypothesized that if any group of women was to reject sex role stereotypes,

college women would be most likely to do so. A group of
74 college men and 80 college women completed the 122-
item Sex Role Questionnaire three times. The first two
times the questionnaire was completed under male and
female directions respectively, and the third time the
students marked what they thought were themselves. Thus,
for each student there was a masculine, feminine and
self-concept score. The result of the Rosenkrantz study
indicated that sex role stereotypes were defined clearly,
and there was a surprising level of agreement among the
groups of college men and women as to these stereotypes.
Both college men and women agreed that the masculine
characteristics were more socially desirable than the
feminine ones. In addition, the self-concepts of college men and women were very similar to their respective
stereotypes. Rosenkrantz et al. (1968) concluded that
the factors which produced the self-incorporation of the
female stereotype, along with its negative valuation,
must be enormously powerful since these college women
were enlightened, carefully selected females who in
general were at least the intellectual equals of their
male peers.

Lunneborg (1970) administered the Edwards Personality Inventory to college students, asking them to predict the answers most men (or women) would give. These
stereotyped instructions resulted in exaggerated existing

sex differences on eight scales and created differences on five scales that males and females normally did not acknowledge. The sex of the student made no difference in the assessment; males described females in the same way as females described other females.

Deutsch and Gilbert (1976) found that women's sex role concepts regarding real and ideal self and their beliefs about what men desire were highly dissimilar. Conversely, males' perceptions in the same area were quite congruent. Deutsch and Gilbert reported that the average college undergraduate woman's self-concept was that she was slightly feminine, desiring to be more androgenous, but believing she would be more desirable to males if she behaved in a more feminine manner. The same researchers suggested that the acquisition of masculine traits by females might be adjustive in the social context of a male-oriented culture. Males do not need to adopt feminine traits to be adjusted to a masculine society. The authors expressed hope that counselors would avoid biases that would result in keeping the woman client "in her place" when "her place" might include maladjustment and dissatisfaction.

Counselors and Sex Role

Just as sex role research has concentrated on the female, the majority of studies examining counselors and sex role stereotyping also has centered on the female counselee. The American Psychological Association (Brodsky & Holroyd, 1975) in a <u>Report of the Task Force on Sex Bias and Sex Role Stereotyping in Psychothera-peutic Practice</u> warns that "at a minimum the therapist must be aware of his own values and not impose them on his patients. Beyond that, they have a responsibility for evaluating the mental health implications of these values" (p. 1169).

Thomas (1967) researched counselors' perceptions of acceptance, appropriateness of vocational goals and need for further counseling for female clients who showed interests in traditionally masculine (deviate) goals compared to females who showed interest in femin-ine (conforming) vocational goals. His subjects were 62 secondary school counselors in suburban St. Paul, Minnesota. Thomas reported that female counselors showed a greater acceptance toward all clients than did male counselors, regardless of the purported vocational goal. Male counselors perceived a higher need for coun-seling for all clients. This need for additional coun-seling was less affected by the addition of vocational choice. All counselors rated conforming goals as more appropriate for females; and furthermore, female clients with deviate goals were perceived as needing more coun-seling than those with conforming goals.

Schlossberg and Pietrofesa (1973) reported that both men and women counseling practicum students expressed negative bias toward female clients who considered entering a nontraditional occupational field. The counselors made more negative statements to clients who aspired to male-dominated vocations, and their negative comments centered around the masculinity of the occupation chosen by the deviate female clients.

Smith (1973) disputed Schlossberg and Pietrofesa's methodology and Smith (1974) reported that there was no significant sexual or ethnic discrimination among counselors in her study. She asked secondary school counselors to predict academic success and to choose an appropriate career for four hypothetical cases. Variations in client sex and ethnic designation did not produce variations in counselor evaluations. The sex of the counselors was not related to any pattern or systematic variance in evaluation. Abramowitz, Weitz, and Schwartz (1975), however, confirmed the assertion that counselor bias exists against women entering masculine fields. Their research indicated that the more experienced and traditional counselors exhibited greater levels of prejudice. In fact, traditional counselors relied more on assessments of maladjustment in their counseling of clients, regardless of sex, to explain the clients' problems.

Bingham and House (1974) surveyed counselors' attitudes and factual knowledge of women and work. They found no difference between older and younger counselors' knowledge of factual items. However, younger counselors expressed a slightly more favorable attitude about women assuming a working role in conjunction with homemaking. Women counselors were better informed and had more favorable attitudes about women and work.

Hill (1975) reported that inexperienced counselors, both male and female, were more empathic and elicited more of the clients' feelings with same-sex clients. She hypothesized that when counselors are in training they feel better able to identify with persons whose experiences are similar to their own. With opposite-sex clients, inexperienced counselors talked more about their own feelings. Experienced counselors (both male and female) paired with same-sex clients concentrated more on clients' feelings and were more empathic. These same counselors paired with opposite-sex clients were more directive and active. Hill reported that prior to counseling, most clients preferred male counselors, perhaps due to the expectation of authority and prestige. However, after having received therapy, clients of female counselors expressed more satisfaction with their counseling session than clients of male counselors. The results of the study indicated that the most empathic,

active and satisfying counselors were experienced
females and inexperienced males. Hill suggests that
perhaps females need to gain experience before they feel
confident in their skills. Males may lose interest in
counseling skills, once acquired, and may move on to
other areas of interest, more suited to sex role activities, such as administration and research.

Ahrons (1976) used 204 males and 85 female public
school counselors as subjects to determine if there
were differences in the perceptions of career images of
women. She reported that the male and female counselors
showed no significant difference in their perceptions.
The "career man" concept clustered similarly to other
male concepts, while the "career woman" concept did not
cluster with other female concepts. Thus, inferentially,
the counselors perceived career goals as incompatible
with the traditional feminine roles of wife and mother.
The counselors expected females to experience conflict
in their vocational choices. Because of the congruency
of the male concepts, however, the counselors did not
expect males to experience any such conflict. The
author concluded that women still were considered deviate if they chose not to adhere to the traditional feminine role.

Donahue and Costar (1977) reported that counselors
discriminated in career selections for women. The

researchers investigated 300 high school counselors in Michigan. Half of the subjects were males and half females. Two forms of six case studies were presented to the counselors. The only difference in the forms was that one presented a woman client while the other depicted a male client. For each case study, the subjects were asked to select the most appropriate occupation from a list of 28 possibilities. The counselors chose different occupations for the male and female case studies. The occupations chosen for the female were lower paying, more supervised and required less education. Neither the age nor the sex of counselor appeared statistically significant, but the interaction of age and sex was significant. Female counselors over 40 years old discriminated the most. Males over 40 years of age discriminated least. Females under 40 discriminated less than males under 40. Another significant factor was the size of the community where the counselor worked: The larger the population of the community, the less the discrimination.

Women constitute the majority of those receiving psychiatric therapy, both in hospitals and outpatient facilities (Levin, Kamin & Levin, 1974; Chesler, 1972). Chesler (1972) suggested that the consistently higher rates of mental illness for females and the higher number of diagnoses of non-sex-linked mental illness may be a function of a diagnostic bias by mental health professionals. It is possible that the therapist's preconceived notions may influence labeling and promote the high incidence of observed mental illness in women (Wesley, 1975). Chesler (1971) maintained that females diagnosed as neurotics were really victims of societal demands and discriminations. She reported that these women were neither "sick" nor "mentally ill," and that both marriage and therapy are socially approved institutions that maintain control over women.

Chesler (1972) interviewed 60 women about their experiences in psychiatric hospitals and private outpatient therapy. She concluded that in psychotherapy, women are rewarded for dependent behavior and are encouraged to adopt traditional female stereotypes. She suggested that clinicians, most of whom are men, treated their clients, most of whom are women, as "wives" or "daughters" rather than as people. They reinforced the traditionally feminine characteristics of dependence, submission and acceptance. Women's inability to adjust to feminine roles has been considered as a deviation from "natural" female psychology rather than an indication of the impropriety of such stereotyping.

An opinion article by Houck (1972) in the American Journal of Psychiatry on how to manage the "intractable female patient" presents a graphic example of how female

psychology is interpreted by male professionals stereotypically. This intractable female patient "is not
easily governed, managed or directed; obstinate; not
easily manipulated or wrought; not easily relieved or
cured" (p. 27). Houck reported that this type of patient
wants to be controlled and it is the doctor's duty to
control her. Houck also proposed that the most important part of the treatment was to help the husband assume
control of the family and the female client. Houck
associated mental illness with a woman's inability (or
refusal) to function in the stereotypic role.

The differential valuations of behaviors and characteristics stereotypically ascribed to men and women
are well established. Masculine traits often are perceived as more socially desirable than feminine traits.
Kogan, Quinn, Ax and Ripley (1957) reported that a high
correlation (< .89) exists between the variable of (psychological) health-sickness, and the variables of social
desirability. Social desirability had a greater influence
on personality assessment than any other factor related
to the kinds of people. Findings by Kogan et al. (1957)
were based on data provided by Q sorts of 24 hospital-
ized adult male psychiatric patients and 24 male university students screened and assessed as having no
psychiatric difficulties. Each item was classified as to
its personality variable by six clinicians who served as

judges. The clinicians also sorted the Q array with respect to health-sickness and social desirability variables. The variable described as health-sickness was indistinguishable from social desirability.

Cowen (1961) related social desirability to different concepts of mental health and found that the social desirabilities of behavior related to "normality-abnormality" are correlated. Those behaviors that college students considered to be of low social desirability correlated positively with how clinicians conceptualized abnormality. Cowen warns that social desirability stereotypes contaminate clinicians' assessment of normality. Weiner, Blumberg, Sigman and Cooper (1959), using a Q sort, found a high correlation between concepts of social desirability and adjustment. Social acceptability of a person's behavior seems to be a major determinant in assessing a level of adjustment.

Aslin (1974) reported that there was a significant relationship between psychotherapists' judgement of mental health and social desirability. She stated that the socially desirable pole equaled the description of the mental health pole. Counselors who perceived themselves as helping clients free themselves from sex role stereotypes judged mentally healthy males and females in similar terms. However, those counselors who were not committed specifically to working with women and stereotypes judged women differently from men or nonsex specified adults.

The relationship between social desirability and concepts of mental health gains more importance when the relationship between social desirability and masculine, as opposed to feminine characteristics, also is considered. As reported earlier, a study by Broverman et al. (1970) has become a landmark in the area of clinical perceptions of sex role stereotyping. These researchers hypothesized that clinicians would maintain parallel distinctions in their concept of what, behaviorally, is healthy or pathological when considering men versus women and that the clinical judgements about the traits characterizing healthy mature individuals will differ as a function of the sex of the person judged.

The subjects for this study were 79 clinically trained psychologists, psychiatrists and social workers (46 men, 33 women) who functioned in clinical settings. The ages varied between 23 and 55 and their experience ranged from internship to extensive professional practice.

The subjects were given the Sex Role Questionnaire with one of three sets of instructions: "male," "female" or "adult." The "male" instructions stated "think of a normal, adult man and then indicate on each item the pole to which a mature, healthy, socially

competent adult man would be closest." The "female" and
"adult" instructions differed in that the words "woman"
and "adult" were substituted for the word "man."
Responses to the adult instructions were considered indicative of ideal health patterns, without respect to sex.
The subjects were asked to consider opposing poles of
each item as direction rather than extremes of behavior.

$\underline{T}$ tests were used to compare scores of male clinicians and female clinicians. None of the tests was significant. Both the male and female clinicians agreed on
the behaviors and attributes characteristic of a healthy
man, a healthy woman and a healthy adult independent of
sex; and these assessments parallelled the sex role
stereotypes prevalent in society. They found that clinicians' concepts of a healthy man did not differ significantly from their concept of a healthy adult. However,
their concept of a healthy woman did differ significantly
from their concept of a healthy adult. It was determined that, from the viewpoint of societally acceptable
behavior, a woman must accept the norms of her sex even
though these behaviors are considered, in general, to be
less socially desirable and less healthy for the nonsex
specifically competent mature adult.

Neulinger, Schillinger, Stein and Welkowitz (1970)
reported differences in the responses of 114 therapists
to questions about the optimally integrated persons.

Analyses of a personality questionnaire based on Murray's need system revealed that female therapists described achievement as more necessary for men than for women. Male therapists rated abasement as more necessary for women than did female therapists. In general, the subjects rated dominance, achievement, autonomy, aggression and counteraction as more indicative of mental health in men than in women; while patience, nurturance, play, deference, succorance and abasement were rated as greater needs for the optimally integrated females than for males.

Nowacki and Poe (1973) investigated the generalizability of the Broverman et al. (1970) findings that there is a difference in the concept of mental health for a male and a female. They administered both the Sex Role Questionnaire and the Poe and Matias Semantic Differential to college students. On both scales they reported a difference between the mean rating for a mentally healthy male and female; they also found a difference between the rating made by male and female college students. This latter result is different from the Broverman et al. findings.

Lewittes, Moselle and Simmons (1973) studied sex role biases in clinical assessments based on Rorschach interpretations of 22 male and 22 female psychologists who indicated projective tests as one of their areas of interest. Each subject received the same Rorschach protocol; half the subjects were told that the protocol was of a 26-year old female and half were told that it was of a 26-year male. When the psychologists were judging degree of pathology or intellectual functioning, no difference was found. However, both sexes tended to be biased in favor of their own sex when making clinical judgements. Compared to the Broverman et al. (1970) study, female clinicians in the Lewittes, Moselle, and Simmons (1973) study demonstrated greater pro-female bias, while male clinicians showed less negative female bias.

Goldberg (1973) studied the attitudes towards women of 184 urban practicing clinical psychologists. All subjects completed questionnaires concerning attitudes toward men and women in general, the mental health standards for men and women and the mental health standards for adults in general. Also investigated were the subjects' attitudes towards men and women who needed psychotherapy. The data were analyzed according to age, sex and experience level of the subjects. While the results did not reveal markedly prejudicial sex-linked attitudes, differences appeared between some groupings. Younger female therapists were the least likely to express the traditional view of women while older male therapists were most likely to maintain the traditional female

stereotype. Women therapists, in general, perceived
men and women more equally than male therapists.
Goldberg concluded that the expressed attitudes of clinical psychologists toward men and women are multifaceted
and complex and that simple statements of unqualified
prejudice against women among this population were
unfounded.

Duplicating the Broverman et al. (1970) study with
90 counselors "in training" (45 male and 45 female),
Maslin and Davis (1975) found that males continued to
maintain somewhat more stereotypic standards of mental
health for females than for males or adults. Female
counselors "in training" perceived all healthy persons
similarly regardless of sex. Maslin and Davis confirmed
the Broverman et al. (1970) findings that professional
concepts of mental health for adults were in accord with
nonprofessional ideas of socially desirable traits. However, unlike subjects in the previous research, males and
females disagreed in their expectations of healthy
females. One possible explanation cited was that the
feminist movement has had a greater effect on women than
men.

Fabrikant (1974) supported the Broverman et al.
(1970) findings of a double standard of mental health for
men and women. Male characteristics were considered to
be positively valued while female characteristics had a

negative value. Fabrikant concluded that patients and
therapists alike maintained many of the same stereotypes, and women who accepted female stereotypes for
themselves found that they behaved in norms that were
substandard for mature adults. However, there was some
change in the traditional preference of women for men
as their therapists (Fabrikant, 1974). Simons and Helms
(1976) reported most college women preferred male counselors; but when the counselors stated that their
specialty was women's problems, female counselors were
preferred. Women therapists perhaps would understand
better the needs of women clients.

Cowan (1976) studied sex roles associated with
problems in therapy rather than those associated with
judgements of healthy persons. She mailed the Broverman
Sex Role Questionnaire to 115 psychologists and asked to
what extent they thought one of two poles represented a
greater problem for the female client and to what
extent, for the male client. Thus, a client who had a
high score on feminine traits would be viewed as being
too feminine. She found the adult standards were being
applied to women. Women in therapy were considered too
feminine. However, male problems were not assessed on
the sex role dimension. The possibility that male problems might result from being too masculine was not indicated. Therapists suggested that female-valued traits

such as gentleness and tact were problems for female
clients. Women in therapy were too gentle, tactful,
etc. Therefore, it cannot be concluded that because
healthy females are expected to be less independent
and aggressive than the healthy male, therapists perceive female clients as too independent and too aggressive and want them to become more dependent and passive.

Billingsley (1977) investigated the extent to
which a pseudo-client's sex and the presenting problem
influenced the treatment goal choices of practicing male
and female therapists. She reported that the male and
female therapists chose different treatment goals for
the client with the males choosing more feminine treatment goals and vice versa. She concluded that the main
considerations in choosing treatment goals were the
client's pathology and the counselor's sex, and that
client's sex was only a secondary consideration.

Meanwhile, Hill, Tanney and Leonard (1977) reported
that high school counselors' reactions to female clients
varied according to age, problem type, client's age and
counselor sex. As compared to women with vocational/
educational problems, women with personal/social problems were considered as having more problems, able to
profit more from counseling, desirable to work with,
needing more counseling and receiving more empathy.
In general, counselors perceived that older women needed

more support than younger ones. Female counselors found younger women experiencing existential anxiety more serious than older women experiencing anxiety. Male counselors did not differentiate according to age. When treating two educational/vocational decisions, one being traditional and one nontraditional, the counselors perceived no difference in dilemmas. This contrasts sharply with Thomas and Stewart (1971) who reported that counselors perceived women wanting nontraditional careers as having the greater problem.

There are little data available on how sex role stereotyping specifically affects the counseling situation. Some indications of differential treatment were found by Fabrikant (1974) who reported that female patients were in therapy more than twice as long as male patients. Fabrikant concluded that "the overall results most strongly support the feminist viewpoint that females in therapy are victimized by a social structure and therapeutic philosophy that keeps them dependent for as long as possible" (p. 96).

Sex role stereotyping can prove detrimental to men in therapy as well as women. What often draws men to the counseling situation is an opportunity to express aspects of their sexuality not readily reinforced in other areas (Nelson & Segrist, 1975). If the counselor also perceived the traditional stereotype as desirable, male clients may experience further rejection. To the extent that women must become increasingly liberated from their roles, it is required that to the same degree, men must discover new ways of being (Ferreira, 1974). Only if a male can consider it safe to expose his complete self to his peers, can he begin to translate his whole self into daily behavior.

Summary

The amount of literature concerning sex role research has been increasing, but results have been inconclusive. Before 1970, men and women were presumed to have different personality characteristics and any deviance from the assigned role was opposed vigorously by society as a whole and counselors in particular. Mental health was considered a successful adjustment to one's environment, and it was reported that the early acquisition of gender identity would promote this adjustment. However, recent research has indicated some potential disadvantages to sex role identification.

Because the male stereotype tends to be regarded more positively, it is not surprising that the research has shown women to have more negative self-concepts than men. Sex role stereotyping has repressed and confused the vocational aspirations of females, caused psychic conflict regarding achievement and mental health, and

has contributed to devaluation by females of their sex
(Maslin & Davis, 1975).

Despite the avowed commitment by the helping profession to the goal of optimal development of each individual, mental health professionals have reinforced sex
role stereotyping. Their past perceptions have delineated
separate characteristics for men and women. Counselors
have had negative reactions to counselees who have not
conformed to the appropriate sex role stereotype.

Community college counselors may practice sex role
stereotyping similar to that prevalent in society. On
the other hand, it may be that the traditional social
desirability represented by the positive evaluation of
male characteristics is being replaced by the recogni-
tion among therapists of the harm which may occur when
clients are sexually stereotyped. Only through current
investigations can this be determined.

CHAPTER III
RESEARCH METHODOLOGY

This study was accomplished through a descriptive
or exploratory method of research which compared sys-
tematically how male and female community college counselors perceive males and females, compared to nonsex
specified adults. In addition, it was the degree of
the relationship that would have been determined, if any
correlation existed between the age of counselors and
their perceptions of sex role stereotypes. The purpose
of a descriptive study is to accumulate a data base or
describe phenomena. It does not necessarily explain
relationships or make predictions.

Description of the Sample

The subjects for this study were counselors from
southeastern urban community colleges. As mentioned in
Chapter I, it was felt that the impact of the women's
movement would be stronger in the urban areas; and if
change had begun to occur, it would manifest itself
first in urban areas. Donahue and Costar (1977)
reported that high school counselors who worked in urban
areas attributed higher esteem to women and were less
likely to discriminate.

For this study a community college was defined as a public two-year institution offering comprehensive programs at the freshman and sophomore levels. These community colleges offered, in addition, various technical, occupational and diploma and other nondegree programs. As indicated in Chapter I, this research was limited to the community colleges located in urban areas of the states of Alabama, Georgia, Florida, Mississippi, North Carolina, South Carolina and Tennessee (Appendix F). An area was considered urban if it was a large Standard Metropolitan Statistical Area (SMSA), as defined by the U.S. Department of Commerce, Bureau of the Census (1977). A large SMSA is a metropolitan area with an estimated population of 200,000 or more as of July 1, 1975. Of the 159 large SMSA's in the United States, 30 are located in the seven southeastern states selected for this research; and 29 community colleges are located within these 30 areas.

For the purpose of this study, a counselor was defined as a person working full time for the community college student affairs department. The counselors had to have at least a master's degree and spend at least 50% of their workload in either face-to-face relationships with students or in consultation with other personnel about students. An administrator in each of the community colleges was asked to provide a list of the counselors satisfying the above criteria. By this method, 195 counselors were identified and mailed the sex role questionnaires, a demographic questionnaire and a cover letter (Appendix D). The acceptable number of usable questionnaires for statistical purposes was set at 100. Of the 195 questionnaires disseminated, 167 (85.6%) were returned and of these 149 (76.4%) were usable. Eleven subjects were eliminated because they did not meet the counselor criteria specified. Therefore, there were 184 counselors meeting the criteria. Another seven subjects were eliminated because they did not complete correctly the questionnaire. There were 87 male counselors and 62 female counselors whose questionnaires were usable (80.9% of the actual number of counselors who met the criteria).

Data Collection

A letter (Appendix A) was sent to the appropriate administrator at each college to explain the study and ask permission to conduct this research at his institution. The administrator was asked to designate one person (the "contact person") to be responsible for the dissemination and collection of the questionnaires. The number of counselors meeting the criteria listed above was requested; a stamped, self-addressed post card was provided (Appendix A). If a community college did not respond within one month, a follow-up letter was sent (Appendix B). The telephone was used as an additional method to improve data collection. The length of time for data collection originally had been set for six weeks; but since this research spanned a time when many colleges were closed for spring break, total data collection time was extended to two months.

Of the 29 community college administrators contacted, 23 responded affirmatively and the counselors on their staff participated in this study. One community college administration refused participation and five never responded.

The contact person was mailed Sex Role Questionnaires equal to the number of counselors designated on the staff, a cover letter (Appendix C) which included directions for the dissemination and collection of the questionnaires, and a stamped, self-addressed envelope for return of the questionnaires.

The Sex Role Questionnaires were stacked alternately by male, female and adult instructions so that each institution received an equal number of questionnaires with each of the three instructions. Each counselor completed only one form of the questionnaire.

Attached to the Sex Role Questionnaire was a letter of introduction and a cover sheet (Appendix D) which included a request for demographic data. The demographic information requested was:

1. today's date;

2. sex of the counselor;

3. date of birth of the counselor;

4. marital status;

5. highest level of education;

6. date of last degree;

7. major areas of study for last degree; and

8. percent of work day spent in face-to-face relationships with students or with other personnel concerning students.

The counselors were not told the purpose of this research. There was no attempt to disguise the sex of the investigator because Field (1975) reported that, in sex role research, the sex of the investigator had no effect on either response rate or response bias.

It was requested that the completed questionnaires be returned within two weeks. Three weeks after the mailing of the questionnaires, a follow-up call was made to the contact person at each institution that had not returned the questionnaires.

Instrumentation

The development of the instrument used in this research, the 36-item form of the Sex Role Questionnaire

produced by Rosenkrantz et al. (1968), has been presented in Chapter II. The Sex Role Questionnaire had
been employed successfully in many studies (Broverman
et al., 1970; Nowacki & Poe, 1973; Cowan, 1976).

The instrument was designed to provide indices of
current attitudes or perceptions. That the questionnaire
taps meaningful dimensions is attested to by a high consistency of responses from individuals of diverse backgrounds with respect to how they perceive men and women.
Individual differences in perceptions of sex differences
and self-concepts relate positively to such variables
as plans to seek education beyond college, plans to
combine employment with child rearing and maternal
employment (Broverman, Vogel, Broverman, Clarkson &
Rosenkrantz, 1972).

The items are classified as to which pole is
judged more socially desirable (Appendix E). On the
basis of previous studies, the female pole was judged
more socially desirable on 12 items. These female-
valued items compose a constellation which centers on
interpersonal warmth and emotional expressions and
includes such items as "tactful," "easily expressed
tender feelings" and "gentle." Earlier studies
(Rosenkrantz et al., 1968) indicated that these traits
were used more often to describe women than men.

The remaining 24 items form a cluster of traits that reflect competency. Included in the "competency cluster" are such attributes as independence, ambition, aggression and logic. In previous studies it was determined that these traits were perceived more often as characterizing men than women (Rosenkrantz et al., 1968).

To explore further the dimensions reflected by the stereotypic items, factor analyses were performed separately on the masculinity and femininity responses in both a sample of men and a sample of women (Broverman et al., 1972). Each of the six analyses produced two initial factors which accounted for an average of 61% of the total extractable communality. In each of the analyses, the first factor consisted of these stereotypic items on which the male pole had been designated the more socially desirable, while the second factor consisted of items on which the female pole was the more socially desirable. The results indicated that the male-valued items and the female-valued items constitute two orthogonal, independent dimensions of the stereotype.

Each of the 36 items on the questionnaire is presented in bipolar form and is scored on a 60-point scale ranging from 10 to 70. To aid in the analyses of the data, the scores for the items which represent the socially desirable pole that have a score of 10 were

transformed so that a high score always meant a more
socially desirable score.

No individual male or female score has any special
meaning. The mean of scores in the adult instructions
was the norm against which the male and female scores
are judged. This is based on the assumption that what
counselors consider to be healthy, mature, socially competent for an adult (regardless of sex) reflects an
ideal standard. Male and female scores which did not
differ significantly from the mean of the adult were
considered to be representative of healthy, mature,
socially competent individuals. In addition to the Sex
Role Questionnaire, the counselors were asked to complete the cover sheet which included requests for demographic data.

Data Analysis

The data collection process, previously described,
yielded two basic groupings of data: demographic variables and Sex Role Questionnaire scores. This research
focused on the demographic variables of sex and age of
the community college counselors and the relationship
each had to the perceptions of the male, female and
adult.

Broverman et al. (1970) employed t tests to analyze their data. However, this procedure has been

criticized because the use of t̲ tests with multiple

comparisons often leads to excessive error rates

(Johnson & Jones, 1972). The error rate, using multiple

t̲ tests, can increase to the point where the results

of the whole experiment become untenable. Consequently,

a preferable multiple comparison test is an analysis of

variance (ANOVA):

> Multiple t̲ tests carried out on the same
> data . . . overlap in the information they
> provide and it is not easy to assess the
> evidence for over-all existence of import-
> ance of treatment effects from a complete
> set of such differences . . . . ANOVA
> packages the information in the data into
> neat, distinct "bundles," permitting a rel-
> atively simple judgement to be made about
> the effects of the experimental treatments.
> (Hays, 1963, p. 143)

The major concern of this research was to learn

what were counselors' perceptions of the male, the

female, and the adult and whether male and female coun-

selors' perceptions of males, females and adults differed

significantly. The data scores gleaned from the Sex Role

Questionnaire and the demographic data were analyzed,

using a 2 x 3 factorial design. The dependent variables

in a factorial design are arranged so that the effects of

each independent variable on the dependent variable are

assessed separately from every other independent variable

(Myers & Grossen, 1974). Each independent variable is

called a main variable. The term "main effect" refers to

a significant difference between the mean of one or more

levels of a main variable and the grand mean for that
variable. The joint effect of two or more independent
variables on a dependent variable is called an interaction. To test the main effects, as well as the interaction effects, a 2 x 3 completely randomized analysis of
variance was performed on the raw scores (Kirk, 1968).
Figure 1 is a diagram of this procedure.

                    MI   FI   AI

    MC

    FC

    MI--Instructed to describe males
    FI--Instructed to describe females
    AI--Instructed to describe adults
    MC--Male Counselors
    FC--Female Counselors

        Figure 1. 2 x 3 Randomized Analysis of Variance

        If the preliminary analysis of variance had shown
overall significance, a Newman-Keuls post hoc comparison
would have been performed (Ferguson, 1976, pp. 297-300).
The Newman-Keuls method uses the criterion that the
probability of rejecting the null hypothesis when it is
true should not exceed .01 or .05 for all ordered pairs,
regardless of the number of steps they are apart. A
comparison at the 95% confidence interval would be considered significant.

To determine if any correlation exists between counselors' ages and counselors' perceptions of sex role stereotypes, a Pearson r was performed. The use of the Pearson r assumes that the population is symmetrical, linear, unimodel; that both variables have been randomly sampled from normally distributed populations and that these populations have similar variances (Myers & Grossen, 1974). The sample in this study satisfied these criteria. Having calculated the Pearson r, the results were tested for significance at the .05 level.

No attempt was made to analyze the scores on the individual items in the Sex Role Questionnaire beyond the computation of the mean, variance and standard deviation for each of the items on each set of instructions. These data are available in Appendix G for use in any later investigation.

Limitations

Since a deliberate sample limited to southeast urban community college counselors was selected for this study rather than a random sample from the entire universe of community college counselors, the generalizability of results should be limited to urban community college counselors. Furthermore, the geographic representation may limit the external validity of the results obtained.

A second limitation lies in the instrumentation. Because the counselors were asked to complete the Sex Role Questionnaire, they were required to describe the adult, male or female, with respect to only those dimensions represented on the questionnaire. Consequently, if the counselors' perception of the male, female or adult included attributes other than those in the questionnaire, this information was not available to the researcher. The results of this study will be specific to the instruments used.

CHAPTER IV
RESULTS

This chapter presents the data gathered by the Sex Role Questionnaire and the demographic questionnaire and discusses their treatment and analysis. Hypothesis I was concerned with differences in perceptions between male and female counselors of males, females and adults. The analysis of variance, presented in Table 1, provides an overall view of the findings.

An inspection of Table 1 reveals that the main effect of sex was not found to be significant. Also there was no significant difference ($p < .05$) in the means of groups receiving male, female and adult instructions on the Sex Role Questionnaire. Because there was no significant F ratio for either of the main effects, no post hoc comparison was performed.

A further inspection of Table 1 reveals that the F ratio for the interaction between sex and perceptions of males, females and adults was significant at $p < .05$. Since the interaction was significant, the further analysis of the simple main effects was required.

TABLE 1

ANALYSIS OF VARIANCE

Source	SS	df	MS	F	PR F Probability
Sex (S)	5198.50	1	5198.50	.25	.6199
Instructions (I)	41396.86	2	20698.43	.98	.3765
S x I	254623.45	2	127311.73	6.05*	.0030
Error	3009373.47	143	21044.56	----	-----
Total	3310592.308				

*p < .05

Table 2 indicates the differences in the mean scores of female and male counselors for each set of instructions. When instructed to describe the male, male counselors scored higher than female counselors. However, when female counselors were instructed to describe the female and adult, they scored higher than the male counselors. To find out whether the male and female counselors' perceptions of the male, female and adult differed significantly, further analysis of the simple main effects was done.

TABLE 2

MEAN SCORES

	MI	FI	AI	
MC	1601.60	1499.34	1486.66	1528.75
FC	1502.00	1544.78	1585.63	1540.74
TOTAL	1555.63	1530.39	1515.33	

Relative to Hypothesis II, the results of Simple Main Effect are shown in Table 3. Each of the interactions was tested at a level of .01 (total error rate of .03), and none of the interactions was significant. Each of the interactions was also tested at α levels of .05 (total error rate of .15); two of the interactions were significant. There was a significant interaction between

male and female counselors in their perceptions of the
male and also a significant difference between male and
female counselors in their perceptions of the adult.

TABLE 3

SIMPLE MAIN EFFECT

Source	SS	MS	df	F
Sex at MI	128215.59	128215.59	1	6.09*
Sex at FI	25432.32	25432.32	1	1.21
Sex at AI	103855.35	103855.35	1	4.94*
within groups	3009373.47	21044.59	143	

α .05,1,143=3.92

α .01,1,143=6.70

Hypotheses III and IV were concerned with the correlation between ages of the counselors and their perceptions of males and females on the Sex Role Questionnaire. It should be noted that on those questionnaires
dealing with perceptions of the male five respondents
(one male, four female) failed to indicate their ages;
on those questionnaires dealing with perceptions of the
female, two respondents (one male, one female) failed to
indicate their ages; and on those questionnaires dealing
with perceptions of the adult, two respondents (two
females) did not indicate their ages.

Table 4 shows that none of the correlations was significant. However, there seemed to be a trend in the direction of the correlation. As the age of male and female counselors increased, the scores relating to perceptions of the male and female decreased. Younger male counselors and older female counselors scored higher on the questionnaires relating to perceptions of the adult, but these results were not significant.

TABLE 4

CORRELATIONS BETWEEN AGE AND SCORE

	MI	FI	AI
MC	-.035	-.07	-.22
FC	-.42	-.28	-.15
TOTAL	-.06	-.21	-.08

An additional Pearson r correlation was performed to see if there was any relationship between years since last degree and score. On the form reporting perceptions of males, two female counselors neglected to report the number of years since their last degree.

Table 5 reveals that there was no significant correlation between years since last degree and score. However, there is some indication that the fewer the years since the completion of the last degree, the higher the score.

TABLE 5

CORRELATION BETWEEN YEARS SINCE LAST
DEGREE AND SCORE

	MI	FI	AI
MC	.24	-.06	-.18
FC	-.25	-.47	-.01
TOTAL	.09	-.21	-.12

One more analysis of the data was performed. For each item on the Sex Role Questionnaire, the mean, variance and standard deviation was determined. This information is included in Appendix G for possible use in later investigations.

CHAPTER V
DISCUSSION

The current study examined the sex role perceptions
of counselors as a function of their expectations of
males, females and adults. This investigation was organized and conducted as outlined in Chapter III; and the
statistical evidence was reported in Chapter IV. Various conclusions relative to the hypotheses stated in
Chapter I may be drawn from the study. These are dis-
cussed below.

Conclusions Drawn from this Investigation

With regard to Hypothesis I, the F ratio associated with the mean scores of groups of counselors
asked to describe the male, female and adult was not
significant. Therefore, one can conclude that there
was no general tendency for either male or female counselors in urban southeastern community colleges to produce consistently, either higher or lower scores, simply
by virtue of a respondent's sex. This finding, in conjunction with the significant interaction of counselors'
sex and their perceptions of male, female and adult,
indicated that any difference in counselors' scores was
due to a differing view of sex role.

67

There was no significant F ratio associated with varying of instructions on the Sex Role Questionnaire; whether a respondent answered the male, female or adult set of instructions did not produce a significant F ratio. Therefore, it appeared that for southeastern urban community college counselors, perceptions of males, females, and adults did not differ from each other. The lack of a significant difference among the male, female and adult scores suggests that the double standard formerly applied in judging social desirability and mental health of males vis-a-vis females may be waning and a new androgynous standard which incorporates both masculine and feminine personality traits may be emerging.

It was not the purpose of this research to investigate whether the positions of the male, female and adult standards were comparable to the results obtained in the Broverman et al. (1970) study. Different statistical procedures were used in two studies. The differences in means reported by Broverman reflect a difference in proportions of subjects selecting one pole of an item over the other pole. The adult standard was represented by that pole of each item on which the majority of subjects completing adult instructions agreed. However, in the present study the items are scored on a continuum from one pole to the other and the means represent a position on that continuum. In the present study there was no significant difference in the means of the scores for male, female and adult instructions; on the other hand, in the Broverman study there was no difference between male and adult scores, but the male/adult scores were significantly different from the female scores.

The shift in position indicated by the present study relative to the sex role expectations for the female represents a significant shift from the traditional stereotypic role. The present study suggests that both males and females are expected by counselors to have characteristics similar to those exhibited by the adult. Thus, both males and females can be expected to be healthy, socially desirable people without needing to assume artificial and separate roles. The counselors have demonstrated flexibility of attitudes, indicating a good prognosis for future change.

The literature offers some plausible explanations for this shift. Lewittes et al. (1973) found in their sample of clinicians that men were less biased against women and women more pro-female than previous studies had found. Steinmann et al. (1963) reported that the ideal woman, delineated by men, was not significantly different than women's self-perceptions. Both sexes had the same ideal image; yet neither sex had an accurate perception of how the other sex felt. The increased publicity on sex role may have communicated this information to both sexes. Broverman et al. (1972) stated that the majority of the socially desirable items of the Sex Role Questionnaire represents a competency cluster. The women's movement has done much to publicize the competencies of women, and this type of popular press had no doubt played a large part in shaping counselors' attitudes. In addition, an increasing number of women are becoming visible in positions of authority. This visibility enhances the perception of the woman as a competent human being. As women are perceived to be more competent, scores on the female instructions of the Sex Role Questionnaire increase.

Another explanation for this shift may be that the requirement to eliminate sexism in counseling practice and procedures is no longer a debate; it is a matter of federal law and counselors may be reminded of that frequently in their job situations. Title IX of the Education Amendments of 1972 to the original Civil Rights Act of 1964 prohibits sex discrimination in any education program or activity receiving federal financial assistance. The pressure to comply with Title IX may have created a situation where changes in behavior brought about changes in perceptions.

It might be useful to note that of the seven subjects who were eliminated because they did not complete correctly the Sex Role Questionnaire, five stated that they held no prior expectations of people. One subject seemed to refer to Title IX by saying, "It is against the law for me to have a prior expectation of a woman before I meet her.". Thus, there seemed to be a sensitivity to sexual discrimination.

Hypothesis II was concerned with the interaction effect between the sex of the counselor and the type of perception (male, female or adult) on the Sex Role Questionnaire. While none of the interactions was significant at $p < .01$, two were significant at $p < .05$. When asked to describe their perceptions of adults and males, there was a significant difference between male and female counselors' scores. When asked to describe their perceptions of adults, female counselors produced higher scores than male counselors. As to their perception of males, male counselors' produced higher scores than female counselors. There were no significant differences between perceptions of females as revealed in the scores of male and female counselors.

As has been noted previously, a high score on the Sex Role Questionnaire indicates a high score in social desirability and mental health. In this research, women counselors demonstrated higher expectations for adults than male counselors. Women counselors may be more aware of the need to be competent as well as being culturally conditioned to be warm and expressive. The women's movement encourages women to set higher standards for themselves. This influence may have generalized to the extent that women counselors are setting higher standards for all people to attain, regardless of the sex. Male counselors may not have been as affected by this movement. This could account for Fabrikant's (1974) findings that both male and female clients would prefer male counselors prior to therapy; but having had therapy, both male and female clients express greater satisfaction with female counselors. If female counselors have more socially desirable perceptions of adults, their mental health standards and expectations are higher. Thus, a self-fulfilling prophecy may occur; and clients (both male and female) may complete therapy feeling more socially desirable and mentally healthy when treated by female counselors.

When asked to describe males, male counselors produced significantly higher scores ($p < .05$) than female counselors. Thus, if a male client is counseled by a female counselor, he would be measured by different expectations than if he were counseled by a male counselor, i.e., the male client. In the past, both male and female counselors reserved the more socially desirable perceptions of the male (Nelson & Segrist, 1973; Bem, 1972; Brown, 1957). Complaints of feminists were first generated on behalf of females. However, it would seem that now consciousness-raising needs to be accomplished for the male counselor as well, so that he can modify the belief that men must maintain superior abilities and accomplishments (Ferreira, 1974) to be mentally healthy or socially desirable.

Again, it should be noted there was no difference between male and female counselors' scores on the questionnaires relating to perceptions of females. Thus, it can be concluded that male and female counselors have congruent perceptions of the female. This becomes even more important when considered along with the results indicating no difference in scores on the three sets of questionnaires. When male and female counselors are considered together, male and female counselors both perceive females similarly to adults and males.

Hypotheses III and IV were concerned with the possible correlation of counselors' age and their perceptions of men, women and adults. There was no significant correlation between counselors' age and their score; however, there did appear to be some directionality to the scores. The tendency was for younger counselors to generate higher scores than older counselors, regardless of whether asked to describe male, female or adult. It had been thought that younger counselors would show more congruence in scoring males, females and adults, while

older counselors would delineate more differences
between male, female and adult. This assumption was
based on the research that younger counselors expressed
a more favorable attitude about women (Bingham & House,
1975). This was, however, not the case for this sample
of counselors. The male, female and adult scores were
not significantly different, regardless of the age of
the counselor. An explanation for this lack of significant difference may be drawn from Ryder (1965), who
reported that when new members enter a population, they
can effect an attitude change for all members of that
population. Perhaps it was the influence of the younger
counselors which accounted for the weakening of stereotypic perceptions of southeastern urban community college
counselors of all ages.

Another explanation may be that the women's movement may have been effective in reaching all segments
of the population. This would concur with Roper and
Labeff (1977) who compared their data with C.
Kirkpatrick's 1936 data concerning feminism and sex roles.
Roper and Labeff reported that in the 40-year span there
has been a general trend toward more egalitarian attitudes. They found that both the older and the younger
generations surveyed at the time were more favorably
disposed toward feminist issues such as economic and
political equality; and while the younger women were

favorably inclined toward domestic equality, both generations had liberalized their attitudes.

Simons and Helms (1976) reported that subjects
generally preferred counselors who were older than they.
College women preferred counselors 35-45 years old while
noncollege women preferred counselors 55-65 years old.
The present study has shown that regardless of the age
of the counselor, there was no significant difference in
their sex role perceptions. Thus, if a client was choosing an age range based on preconceived notions of the
younger counselor being less stereotypic, this notion
was unsupported by this research.

An additional analysis was performed to determine
whether there was any correlation between the number of
years since the counselors received their last degree
and the scores yielded on the Sex Role Questionnaires.
Research had indicated the need for counselor or education programs to take an affirmative stance on eliminating sex bias and sex discrimination (Verheyden-Hilliard,
1977). It was assumed that counselor education students
are required to keep abreast of current thought and
would be more aware of problems caused by stereotyping;
consequently, it was believed that the fewer the number
of years since the last degree, the higher the score
would be. While there was a tendency in that direction,
none of the correlations was significant. The question

arises as to how much additional influence the current counselor education programs are having on their students. Fernberger (1948) in discussing racial and sexual stereotypes, noted that:

> It is not surprising that a purely intellectual appeal should have so little effect in changing such opinions. If such stereotypes are to be eliminated, the appeal must be emotional as well as intellectual. (p. 101)

The women's movement has supplied the emotional appeal, and perhaps that appeal was so pervasive that it significantly amplified the intellectual stimulation provided by the formal preparation of the counselors. Another consideration may be that in this study the counselors were not asked what inservice courses, workshops, seminars or college courses they had participated in recently. While these programs may have been external to any degree, they still may have had an influence on counselors who had received degrees earlier. This factor also might account in part for the lack of significant correlation between the years since the last degree and the scores on the Sex Role Questionnaires. It is suggested that further research investigate this issue.

Summary

The findings of the present study stand in contrast to previous studies. Five major findings emerge: First, counselors do not delineate differences in

perceptions of males, females and adults. This implies
a breakdown of the former stereotypes of the female.
Second, male and female counselors perceive females similarly, but have differing views of the male and adult.
Third, there was no correlation between the age of the
counselor and his or her perceptions of males, females
and adults. Fourth, there was no correlation between
the number of years since the counselor's last degree
and his or her perceptions of sex role stereotypes.

Finally, it can be concluded that sex role stereotypes are not as fixed as earlier studies had indicated,
at least as perceived by community college counselors
in seven southeastern states. Although the study did
not attempt to delineate what factors influenced the
change in counselors' perceptions, the fact that change
has occurred indicates that the various forces at work
are effective and should be encouraged.

Recommendations for Further Study

Because the findings of this study are a departure
from previous research, the results need to be further
investigated. In addition, it would be helpful for
other samples to be taken to ascertain whether these
results are in fact limited to the community colleges
that are included in this study.

Since there is a discrepancy in the method of scoring between this study and the original on which it was based, the investigator recommends replication. Using another instrument (such as the Bem Sex-Role Inventory) might be advantageous to further verify the results (Bem, 1974).

It is hoped that this investigation will prove valuable to counselors and counselor educators in providing a medium through which counselors can examine their attitudes and expectations of clients. Counselor educators should further make available the opportunity for sex role research. Counselors should work for the elimination of stereotypic perceptions within the educational setting in which they are working. All people benefit by the elimination of sex role bias; and if it is the counselors' function to benefit not only their clients but also the social environment in which they work, the elimination of sex-role bias will have a salutary effect on society.

APPENDIX A

SAMPLES OF INITIAL CORRESPONDENCE TO ADMINISTRATOR
OF THE SELECTED COMMUNITY COLLEGE

Initial Letter

Response Postcard to be Enclosed with
Initial Letter

2101 Thunderbird Trail
Maitland, Florida 32751
August 10, 1979

Name of Individual
Dean of Student Services
Community College
Address

Dear

I would appreciate your approval of, and participation in, a study sponsored by the Department of Counselor Education at the University of Florida on community (junior) college counselors' perceptions of sex role
stereotypes. Participation would involve having the
counselors on your staff complete a 36-item Sex Role
Questionnaire and a cover sheet which includes a request
for demographic information. The entire process should
take less than 15 minutes of your counselors' time.

It will be necessary to know the number of counselors on your staff who have at least a master's degree
and spend at least 50% of their workload in face-to-face
relationships with students and/or with other personnel
concerning students.

I request that you designate one person, if not
yourself, to coordinate the dissemination and collection
of the questionnaires. The attached stamped, self-
addressed postcard is provided to ease this process.

Your participation in this study is truly appre-
ciated, and in return I would be glad to share with you
any results I obtain. If you have any questions about
this research, please do not hesitate to write me at the
above address or call me collect at (305) 644-6359.

I am looking forward to hearing from you as soon
as possible.

Sincerely,

(Mrs.) Miriam (Mimi) Hull

Enclosure
APPROVED: Dr. Robert O. Stripling
Distinguished Service Professor
University of Florida

Dr. James Wattenbarger
Professor and Director
Institute of Higher Education
University of Florida

80

Name of Institution _____, 1979

Will you participate in this research? Yes__ No__
If you will participate, please indicate the person
responsible for dissemination and collection of questionnaire Miss Ms.
          Mrs. Mr. Dr. _____
position_____ mailing address_____
_____
Please indicate the number of counselors meeting the
criteria mentioned in the second paragraph of my
letter _____.

                              Thank you

Institution
Mailing Address

                                        STAMP

                    Mrs. Miriam (Mimi) Hull
                    2101 Thunderbird Trail
                    Maitland, Florida 32751

APPENDIX B

SAMPLE OF FOLLOW-UP LETTER SENT TO ADMINISTRATOR
OF SELECTED COMMUNITY COLLEGES

2101 Thunderbird Trail
Maitland, Florida 32751
April 4, 1979

Name of Individual
Dean of Student Services
Community College
Address

Dear

Approximately one month ago, I sent you a letter together with a reply postcard, asking your participation in a project sponsored by the University of Florida, Department of Counselor Education. A copy of that letter is enclosed for your reference.

While the original letter may have come at an inopportune time, since many schools were then on spring break, I would very much appreciate it if you could give your prompt attention to this matter now.

I wish to re-emphasize that participation in this study would entail a maximum of 15 minutes of your counselors' time and the study may be of some significance in community college research.

For your convenience, you may indicate your participation in this study on the form at the bottom of this letter, returning it to me in the enclosed self-addressed envelope.

If you have any questions, please do not hesitate to call me collect at (305) 644-6359. Thank you for your kind consideration.

Sincerely,

Miriam (Mimi) Hull

83

_____, 1979

Will you participate in this research? Yes__ No__
If you will participate, please indicate the person
responsible for dissemination and collection of questionnaires.

   Miss Ms.
   Mrs. Mr. Dr. _____
position_____
mailing address_____

Please indicate the number of counselors meeting the
criteria mentioned in the second paragraph of my
original letter _____.

                    Thank you.

APPENDIX C

SAMPLE OF COVER LETTER SENT TO CONTACT PERSON
EXPLAINING DISSEMINATION AND COLLECTION PROCEDURE

2101 Thunderbird Trail
Maitland, Florida 32751
March 12, 1979

Name of Individual
Title
Community College
Address

Dear

I appreciate your indicated willingness to participate in this study sponsored by the University of Florida,
Department of Counselor Education. Enclosed are questionnaires equal in number to the counselors that you or
your college indicated as having at least master's degrees
and spending at least 50% of their workload time in face-
to-face contact with students or with other personnel
about students. Should you need any additional questionnaires for counselors to complete, please do not hesitate
to request them.

Please distribute the questionnaires in order to
your counselors. (The first counselor receiving the first
one . . . the second counselor receiving the second, etc.).
The counselors do not have to be in any specific order
nor do the questionnaires have to be returned in any order.

Because the questionnaires can be completed in less
than 15 minutes, I would request your urging that the completed questionnaires be returned promptly. I would like
to have them returned to me within 2 weeks. In this
study, the return rate is important so we would appreciate
as many responses as possible. The enclosed stamped
envelope is provided for the return of the questionnaires.

Again, many thanks for your participation and if
you have any questions, please do not hesitate to write
or phone me collect at (305) 644-6359.

Sincerely,

(Mrs.) Miriam (Mimi) Hull

mk
Enclosures
APPROVED: Dr. Robert O. Stripling
           Distinguished Service Professor
           University of Florida

           Dr. James Wattenbarger, Professor & Director
           Institute of Higher Education
           University of Florida

APPENDIX D

CORRESPONDENCE TO COUNSELORS

Letter

Demographic Questionnaire

Dear Community or Junior College Counselor:

I would appreciate your completing the following materials which are important to a study being sponsored by the University of Florida, Department of Counselor Education. The entire process should not take more than 15 minutes of your time.

When you have completed the enclosed questionnaire, please return this entire packet to _____ _____ of your college.

Thank you very much.

Sincerely,

Mrs. Miriam (Mimi) Hull

Enclosure

APPROVED: Dr. Robert O. Stripling
Distinguished Service Professor
University of Florida

Dr. James Wattenbarger
Professor and Director
Institute of Higher Education
University of Florida

Demographic Questionnaire

Today's date _____
                 month/day/year

Thank you for your participation in this research. The following information is being asked for statistical purposes only. It will be used to define the population of this study rather than to single out individuals. Please answer all questions to the best of your knowledge.

Sex: M_____ F_____   Date of Birth_____
                                          month/day/year

Highest level of education: (circle)

Bachelor's; Master's; Specialist; Doctorate; other _____
                                                    please
                                                    specify

Date of last degree_____
                        month/year

Major area of study for last degree_____

Present Job Title_____

Department_____

Indicate the percent of your workload spent in face-to-face relationships with students and/or with other personnel concerning students.

Less than 50%_____ 50% or more_____

Please turn page.

APPENDIX E

SOCIAL DESIRABILITY OF ITEMS

Item #	Male-Valued Items
	Socially desirable pole (= masculine pole)
1	Very aggressive
2	Very independent
5	Very dominant
8	Not at all excitable in a major crisis
9	Not at all excitable in a minor crisis
16	Very skilled in business
20	Feelings not easily hurt
24	Can make decisions easily
25	Never cries
26	Almost always acts as a leader
34	Not at all dependent
11	Very competitive
19	Knows the way of the world
21	Very adventurous
29	Not at all uncomfortable about being aggressive
32	Able to separate feelings from ideas
4	Not at all easily influenced
12	Very logical
15	Very worldly
30	Very little need for security
17	Very direct
27	Very self-confident
31	Very ambitious
36	Very assertive

Item #	Female-Valued Items
	Socially desirable pole (= feminine pole)
3	Very emotional
6	Doesn't hide emotions at all
14	Very gentle
23	Very interested in own appearance
35	Easily expresses tender feelings
7	Very talkative
10	Able to devote self completely to others
33	Enjoys art and literature very much
22	Very religious
28	Never sees self as running the show
18	Very aware of the feelings of others
13	Very tactful

APPENDIX F

COMMUNITY COLLEGES LOCATION IN STANDARD METROPOLITAN
STATISTICAL AREAS

The following are the Standard Metropolitan Statistical Areas in the southeastern states studied, as of July 1, 1975, their population and the community colleges located in the area. Where there are no community colleges listed, there were none located in the area.

ALABAMA

Birmingham (785,000)   Jefferson State Jr.
                                       Lawson State Community

Montgomery (248,000)
Mobile (396,000)   Bishop State Jr.
Huntsville (285,000)

GEORGIA

Atlanta (1,776,000)   Dekalb
                                       Atlanta
                                       Clayton

Augusta, Ga./S.C. (274,000)
Columbus, Ga./Ala. (218,000)
Macon (236,000)   Macon Jr.

FLORIDA

Hollywood/Ft. Lauderdale (807,000)   Broward
Jacksonville (675,000)   Florida Jr.
Lakeland/Winter Haven (263,000)   Polk Community
Melbourne/Titusville/Cocoa (229,000)   Brevard Community
Miami (935,000)   Miami Dade Community
Orlando (579,000)   Valencia Community
Pensacola (264,000)   Pensacola Community
Tampa/St. Petersburg (1,333,000)   Hillsborough Community
West Palm Beach/Boca Raton (349,000)   Palm Beach Jr.

MISSISSIPPI

Jackson (279,000)   Hinds Jr.

NORTH CAROLINA

Charlotte/Gastonia (589,000)	Central Piedmont Community
Fayetteville (226,000)	Fayetteville Tech. Inst.
Greensboro/Winston	
High Point (760,000)	Forsyth Tech. Inst.
Raleigh/Durham (462,000)	Wake Tech. Inst.

SOUTH CAROLINA

Charleston, N. Charleston (362,000)	Trident Tech.
Columbia (361,000)	Midlands Tech.
Greenville/Spartansburg (522,000)	Greenville Tech.
	Spartvanville Tech.

TENNESSEE

Chattanooga/Georgia (390,000)	Chattanooga State Tech.
Johnson City/Kingsport/Bristol, Tenn.-Va.	
Knoxville (428,000)	
Memphis (853,000)	Shelby State Community
Nashville/Davidson (745,000)	Volunteer State Community

APPENDIX G

ITEM ANALYSIS: MEAN, VARIANCE AND STANDARD DEVIATION
OF INDIVIDUAL ITEMS ON SEX ROLE QUESTIONNAIRE FOR
MALE, FEMALE AND ADULT INSTRUCTIONS

TABLE 6

MEAN VARIANCE AND STANDARD DEVIATION OF EACH ITEM
MALE INSTRUCTIONS

Item	Mean	Variance	Standard Deviation
Aggressiveness	47.28	48.32	6.95
Independence	48.69	68.68	8.28
Emotional	37.55	89.89	9.48
Influenced	41.65	111.40	10.55
Dominance	45.32	78.85	8.88
Hiding Emotions	32.76	111.04	10.53
Talkative	44.61	68.00	8.24
Excitable/Major Crisis	39.39	49.83	7.06
Excitable/Minor Crisis	47.21	98.56	9.92
Devote to Others	43.09	131.14	11.45
Competitive	49.00	91.88	9.58
Logical	43.61	132.67	11.51
Tactful	42.19	77.33	8.79
Gentle	38.03	107.25	10.35
Worldly	40.51	116.92	10.81
Business Skill	44.13	66.90	8.17
Direct	42.67	122.46	11.06
Aware of Feelings	41.46	132.95	11.53
Knows World	46.51	84.52	9.19
Feeling Hurt	41.40	78.99	8.88
Adventurous	47.92	103.75	10.18
Religious	42.01	96.84	9.84
Appearance	47.76	109.31	10.45
Decision Making	44.40	119.81	10.94
Cries	45.53	101.90	10.09
Leadership	45.00	84.03	9.16
Self-Confidence	46.82	113.51	10.65

TABLE 6--<u>Continued</u>

Item	Mean	Variance	Standard Deviation
Runs Show	38.30	59.35	7.70
Comfort with Aggression	45.80	93.37	9.66
Security	37.05	143.85	11.99
Ambition	48.40	75.65	8.69
Separate Feelings	42.42	106.40	10.31
Enjoys Art & Literature	41.84	81.46	9.02
Dependence	40.76	73.78	8.59
Express Tender Feelings	39.23	141.005	11.87
Assertiveness	44.53	61.78	7.86

TABLE 7

MEAN VARIANCE AND STANDARD DEVIATION OF EACH ITEM
FEMALE INSTRUCTIONS

Item	Mean	Variance	Standard Deviation
Aggressiveness	42.46	59.38	7.70
Independence	44.16	74.21	8.61
Emotional	41.77	98.74	9.93
Influenced	39.37	91.63	9.57
Dominance	38.25	50.64	7.11
Hiding Emotions	43.55	64.59	8.03
Talkative	44.03	69.99	8.36
Excitable/Major Crisis	35.01	68.20	8.25
Excitable/Minor Crisis	39.90	68.68	8.28
Devote to Others	47.83	105.38	10.26
Competitive	43.75	75.05	8.66
Logical	42.72	86.80	9.31
Tactful	44.20	63.29	7.95
Gentle	47.14	84.99	9.21
Worldly	38.48	71.50	8.45
Business Skill	41.46	75.04	8.66
Direct	43.24	91.73	9.57
Aware of Feelings	48.88	107.68	10.37
Knows World	42.33	101.66	10.08
Feeling Hurt	35.64	116.34	10.78
Adventurous	42.27	93.90	9.69
Religious	45.63	59.97	7.74
Appearance	53.40	98.20	9.91
Decision Making	40.38	100.31	10.01
Cries	35.29	88.70	9.41
Leadership	40.75	47.43	6.88
Self-Confidence	44.11	103.27	10.16

TABLE 7--<u>Continued</u>

Item	Mean	Variance	Standard Deviation
Runs Show	41.55	46.17	6.79
Comfort with Aggression	38.74	84.08	9.17
Security	32.42	100.40	10.02
Ambition	46.16	68.36	8.26
Separate Feelings	39.59	142.05	11.91
Enjoys Art & Literature	48.42	92.17	9.60
Dependence	36.61	74.24	8.61
Express Tender Feelings	45.68	118.25	10.87
Assertiveness	39.53	85.04	9.22

TABLE 8

MEAN VARIANCE AND STANDARD DEVIATION OF EACH ITEM
ADULT INSTRUCTIONS

Item	Mean	Variance	Standard Deviation
Aggressiveness	41.60	57.43	7.57
Independence	48.20	84.55	9.19
Emotional	40.30	35.50	5.95
Influenced	41.09	100.80	10.04
Dominance	41.04	44.18	6.64
Hiding Emotions	36.41	58.58	7.65
Talkative	43.55	41.68	6.45
Excitable/Major Crisis	38.83	99.85	9.99
Excitable/Minor Crisis	44.62	93.76	9.68
Devote to Others	40.20	98.93	9.94
Competitive	45.86	85.21	9.23
Logical	46.46	124.01	11.13
Tactful	45.48	107.20	10.35
Gentle	44.48	71.11	8.43
Worldly	38.90	76.42	8.74
Business Skill	40.51	62.30	7.89
Direct	46.74	112.43	10.60
Aware of Feelings	44.14	178.17	13.34
Knows World	44.37	112.04	10.58
Feeling Hurt	42.14	116.55	10.79
Adventurous	42.44	86.15	9.28
Religious	43.67	46.98	6.85
Appearance	49.46	103.25	10.16
Decision Making	41.16	123.33	11.10
Cries	42.46	71.44	8.45
Leadership	42.53	63.63	7.97
Self-Confidence	45.16	106.52	10.32

101

TABLE 8--Continued

Item	Mean	Variance	Standard Deviation
Runs Show	39.29	43.29	6.58
Comfort with Aggression	41.25	48.43	6.95
Security	32.39	58.72	7.66
Ambition	46.41	79.58	8.92
Separate Feelings	43.00	186.57	13.65
Enjoys Art & Literature	42.27	83.34	9.13
Dependence	41.65	89.51	9.46
Express Tender Feelings	41.14	143.26	11.96
Assertiveness	41.44	69.01	8.30

REFERENCES

Abramowitz, S. T., Weitz, L. J., & Schwartz, J. M. Comparative counselor inferences toward women with medical school aspirations. Journal of College Student Personnel, 1975, 16, 128-130.

Ahrons, C. R. Counselors' perceptions of career images of women. Journal of Vocational Behavior, 1976, 8, 197-207.

Aslin, A. Feminist and community mental health expectations for women. Doctoral dissertation, University of Maryland, 1974.

Astin, H. S. Career development of girls during the high school years. Journal of Counseling Psychology, 1968, 15, 536-540.

Athanassiades, J. R. The internalization of the female stereotype by college women. Human Relations, 1977, 30, 187-199.

Baruch, G. K. The traditional feminine role: Some negative effects. School Counselor, 1974, 21, 284-289.

Bem, S. L. Psychology looks at sex roles: Where have all the androgynous people gone? Paper presented at UCLA Symposium on Women, May 1972.

Bem, S. L. The measurement of psychological androgyny. Journal of Consulting and Clinical Psychology, 1974, 42, 155-162.

Billingsley, D. Sex bias in psychotherapy: An examination of the effects of client's sex, pathology and therapist sex on treatment planning. Journal of Consulting and Clinical Psychology, 1977, 45, 250-256.

Bingham, W. C., & House, E. W. ACES members' attitudes toward women and work. Counselor Education and Supervision, 1974, 14, 204-214.

Brodsky, A., & Holroyd, J. Report of the task force on sex bias and sex role stereotyping in psychotherapeutic practice. American Psychologist, 1975, 30, 1169-1175.

Broverman, I., Broverman, D., Clarkson, F., Rosenkrantz, P., & Vogel, S. Sex role stereotypes and clinical judgments of mental health. Journal of Consulting and Clinical Psychology, 1970, 34, 1-7.

Broverman, I., Vogel, S., Broverman, D., Clarkson, F., & Rosenkrantz, P. Sex role stereotypes: A current appraisal. Journal of Social Issues, 1972, 28, 59-78.

Brown, D. G. Masculinity-femininity development in children. Journal of Consulting Psychology, 1957, 21, 197-202.

Cancian, F. M. Mass media coverage of women: Changes from 1965-1974. Unpublished manuscript. Stanford University, 1975.

Chesler, P. Stimulus/response: Men drive women crazy. Psychology Today, 1971, 8, 18, 22.

Chesler, P. Women and madenss. New York: Doubleday & Co., 1972.

Cowan, G. Therapist judgments of client's sex-role problems. Psychology of Women Quarterly, 1976, 1, 115-124.

Cowen, E. L. The social desirability of trait descriptive terms: Preliminary norms and sex differences, Journal of Social Psychology, 1961, 55, 225-233.

Cox, F. Psychology. Dubuque, Iowa: Wm. C. Brown Company, 1973.

Cross, K. P. College women: A research description. Proceedings of the National Convention of the National Association of Women Deans and Counselors, 1968. (Monograph)

Dellas, M., & Gaier, E. L. The self and adolescent identity in women: Options and implications. Adolescent, 1975, 10, 399-407.

Deutsch, C. J., & Gilbert, L. A. Sex-role stereotypes: Effect on perceptions of self and others and on personal adjustment. Journal of Counseling Psychology, 1976, 23, 373-379.

Donahue, T. J., & Costar, J. W. Counselor discrimination against young women in career selection. Journal of Counseling Psychology, 1977, 24, 481-486.

Fabrikant, B. The psychotherapist and female patient. In V. Franks & Burtle, V. (Eds.). Women in therapy. New York: Brunner Mazel, 1974.

Farmer, S. What inhibits achievement and career motivation in women? Counseling Psychologist, 1976, 6, 12-15.

Ferguson, G. A. Statistical analysis in psychology and education. New York: McGraw-Hill, 1976.

Fernberger, S. W. Persistence of stereotypes concerning sex differences. Journal of Abnormal and Social Psychology, 1948, 43, 97-101.

Ferreira, A. Male dilemma. Contemporary Education, 1974, 46, 68-70.

Field, H. S. Effects of sex of investigator on mail survey response rate and response bias. Journal of Applied Psychology, 1975, 60, 772-773.

Ginzberg, E. Lifestyles of educated women. New York: Columbia University Press, 1966.

Ginzberg, E., & Yohalem, A. M. Educated American women: Self-portraits. New York: Columbia University Press, 1966.

Goldberg, L. H. Attitudes of clinical psychologists toward women. Doctoral dissertation, Illinois Institute of Technology, 1973.

Gordon, F. E., & Hall, D. T. Self-image and stereotype of femininity: Their relationship to women's role conflicts and coping. Journal of Applied Psychology, 1974, 59, 241-243.

Hacker, H. M. The new burdens of masculinity. Marriage and Family Living, 1957, 19, 227-233.

Harrison, J. Changing male roles. Taking sexism out of education. Washington, D.C.: U.S. Government Printing Office, 1978.

Hauts, P. S., & Entwisle, D. R. Academic achievement effort among females: Achievement attitudes and sex role orientation. Journal of Counseling Psychology, 1968, 15, 284-286.

Hays, W. L. Statistics. New York: Holt, Rinehart & Winston, 1963.

Hays, W. L. Statistics for the social sciences. New York: Holt, Rinehart & Winston, Inc., 1973.

Hilgard, E. R., Atkinson, R. C., & Atkinson, R. L. Introduction to psychology. New York: Harcourt, Brace, Jovanovich, Inc., 1975.

Hill, C. E. Sex of client and sex and experience level of counselor. Journal of Counseling Psychology, 1975, 22, 6-11.

Hill, C., Tanney, M. F., & Leonard, M. M. Counselor reactions to female clients: Type of problem, age of client and sex of counselor. Journal of Counseling Psychology, 1977, 24, 60-65.

Hollender, J. Sex differences in sources of social self-esteem. Journal of Counseling and Clinical Psychology, 1972, 38, 343-347.

Houck, J. H. The intractable female patient. American Journal of Psychiatry, 1972, 129, 27-31.

Johnson, R. H., & Jones, L. Multiple comparisons and error rate. Journal of College Student Personnel, 1972, 13, 154-158.

Kirk, R. E. Experimental design: Procedures for the behavioral sciences. Belmont, California: Brooks/ Cole, 1968.

Kirkman, A. V., Jr. For men only. Community and Junior College Journal, 1977, 48, 28-29.

Kogan, W. S., Quinn, R., Ax, A. F., & Ripley, H. S. Some methodological problems in quantification of clinical assessment Q array. Journal of Consulting Psychology, 1957, 21, 57-62.

Komisar, L. The new feminism. Saturday Review, 1970, 52, 27.

Krech, D., Crutchfield, R. S., & Livson, N. Elements of psychology. New York: Alfred A. Knopf, Inc., 1970.

Levin, S. V., Kamin, L. E., & Levin, E. L. Sexism and psychiatry. American Journal of Orthopsychiatry, 1974, 44, 327-337.

Lewittes, D. J., Moselle, J. A., & Simmons, W. L. Sex role bias in clinical judgments based on Rorschach interpretations. Proceedings, 81st Annual Convention, American Psychological Association, 1973, 8, 495-496.

Lunneborg, P. W. Stereotypic aspect in masculinity-femininity measurement. Journal of Consulting and Clinical Psychology, 1970, 34, 113-118.

Lynn, D. B. Sex role and parental identification. Child Development, 1962, 33, 555-564.

Maslin, A., & Davis, J. L. Sex roles stereotyping as a factor in mental health standards among counselors in training. Journal of Counseling Psychology, 1975, 22, 87-91.

Miller, T. O. Male self-esteem and attitudes toward women's roles. Journal of College Student Personnel, 1973, 14, 2-6.

Myers, L. S., & Grossen, N. E. Behavioral research: Theory procedure and design. San Francisco: W. H. Freeman and Co., 1974.

Nelson, R. C., & Segrist, A. E. Boys as persons. Elementary School Guidance and Counseling, 1973, 8, 120-125.

Nelson, R. C., & Segrist, A. E. Raising the male consciousness through the group experience. School Counselor, 1975, 24, 93.

Neulinger, J., Schillinger, K., Stein, M. I., & Welkowitz, J. Perceptions of the optimally integrated person as a function of therapists' characteristics. Perceptual and Motor Skills, 1970, 34, 375-384.

Nowacki, C. M., & Poe, C. A. The concept of mental health as related to sex of person perceived. Journal of Consulting and Clinical Psychology, 1973, 40, 160.

O'Connell, A. N. The relationship between lifestyles and identity synthesis and resynthesis in traditional, neotraditional and nontraditional women. Journal of Personality, 1976, 44, 675-688.

Ohlsen, M. M. Vocational counseling for girls and women. Vocational Guidance Quarterly, 1968, 17, 124-127.

Oliver, L. W. Counseling implications of recent research on women. Personnal and Guidance Journal, 1975, 53, 430-437.

Pietrofesa, J. J., & Schlossberg, N. K. Counselor bias and the female occupational role. Detroit, Michigan: Wayne State University, 1970. (ERIC Document, ED 644-749)

Rieder, C. H. Work, women and vocational education in taking sexism out of education. Washington, D.C.: U.S. Government Printing Office, 1978.

Rogers, C. R. Client centered therapy. Boston: Houghton & Mifflin, 1951.

Roper, B. S., & Labeff, E. Sex roles a feminism revisited: An intergenerational attitude comparison. Journal of Marriage and the Family, 1977, 39, 113-119.

Rose, A. M. The adequacy of women expectations for adult roles. Social Forces, 1951, 30, 60.

Rosen, B., & Jerdee, T. H. Influence of sex role stereotypes on personnel decisions. Journal of Applied Psychology, 1974, 59, 9-14.

Rosen, B., & Jerdee, T. H. The psychological basis for sex role stereotypes: A note on Terborg and Ilg's conclusions. Organizational Behavior and Human Performance, 1975, 4, 151-153.

Rosenkrantz, P., Vogel, S., Bee, H., Broverman, I., & Broverman, D. Sex role stereotypes and self-concepts in college students. Journal of Consulting and Clinical Psychology, 1968, 32, 287-295.

Ryder, H. B. The cohort as a concept in the study of social change. American Sociological Review, 1965, 39, 843-961.

Schlossberg, N. K., & Pietrofesa, J. J. Perspectives in counseling bias: Implications for counselor education. The Counseling Psychologist, 1973, 4, 44-55.

Seltzer, M. M. Contemporary college women view their roles. Journal of College Student Personnel, 1975, 16, 265-269.

Sexton, P. How the American boy is feminized. Psychology Today, 1970, 8, 23-29, 66-67.

Sherriffs, A. C., & Jarrett, R. F. Sex differences in attitudes about sex differences. Journal of Psychology, 1953, 35, 161-168.

Sherriffs, A. C., & McKee, J. P. Qualitative aspects of beliefs about men and women. Journal of Personality, 1957, 25, 451-464.

Simons, J. A., & Helms, J. G. Influence of counselors' marital status, sex and age on college and non-college women's counselors' preferences. Journal of Counseling Psychology, 1976, 23, 380-386.

Smith, M. L. Notes on "Perspectives on counseling bias: Implications for counselor education." Counseling Psychologist, 1973, 4, 93.

Smith, M. L. Influence of client's sex and ethnic group on counselor judgments. Journal of Counseling Psychology, 1974, 2, 516-521.

Steinmann, A., & Fox, D. J. Male-female perceptions of the female role in the United States. The Journal of Psychology, 1966, 64, 265-276.

Steinmann, A., Fox, D. J., & Forkas, R. Male and female perceptions of male sex roles. Proceedings, 76th Annual Convention, American Psychological Association, 1968, 3, 421-422.

Stevens, B. The psychoterapist and women's liberation. Social Work, 1971, 16, 12-18.

Stevens, B. The sexually oppressed male. Psychotherapy Research and Practice, 1974, 11, 16.

Thomas, A. H. Counselor response to divergent vocational goals of a female client. University of Michigan, 1967. Unpublished doctoral dissertation.

Thomas, A. H., & Stewart, N. R. Counselor response to female clients with deviate and conforming career goals. Journal of Counseling Psychology, 1971, 18, 352-357.

Tibbetts, S. L. Sex role stereotyping: Why women discriminate against themselves. Journal of National Association of Women Deans, Administrators and Counselors, 1975, 38, 177-183.

Tibbetts, S. L. Sex role stereotyping and its effects on boys. Journal of the National Association of Women Deans, Administrators and Counselors, 1977, 40, 108-112.

U.S. Bureau of the Census, Statistical Abstract of the United States: 1977 (98th Edition). Washington, D.C., 1977.

Vavrick, J., & Jurick A. P. Self-concept and attitude toward acceptance of females: A note. The Family Coordinator, 1971, 20, 151-152.

Verheyden-Hilliard, M. E. Counseling: Potential superbomb against sexism. American Education, 1977, 13, 12-15.

Weiner, M., Blumberg, A., Sigman, S., & Cooper, A. A judgment of adjustments by psychologists, psychiatric social workers, and college students and its relationship to social desirability. Journal of Abnormal Social Psychology, 1959, 64, 315-321.

Wesley, C. The women's movement and psychotherapy. Social Work, 1975, 20, 120-124.

Wolfe, H. B. An analysis of the work values of women: Implications for counseling. Journal of the National Association of the National Education Association, 1969, 33, 13-18.

Wong, M. R., Davey, J., & Conroe, R. N. Expanding masculinity: Counseling the man in transition. The Counseling Psychologist, 1976, 6, 58-61.

BIOGRAPHICAL SKETCH

Miriam (Mimi) Bernstein Hull was born in
Binghamton, New York, on December 8, 1946. After 13
years her family moved to Rochester, New York, where
she was graduated from Brighton High School in 1964.
Mimi attended Syracuse University in Syracuse, New
York, graduating in 1968 with a B.A. in psychology.
She began graduate work in the counselor education pro-
gram at the University of Florida in Gainesvile,
Florida, where she earned a M.Ed. in 1970. While at
the University of Florida, Mimi was a research assist-
ant for the Institute for the Development of Human
Resources and for the Florida Junior College Inter-
Institutional Research Council. After completing her
doctoral course work in 1971, she accepted a counseling
position at Florida Junior College in Jacksonville,
Florida. There she met her husband, Norman L. Hull.

Mimi had a number of jobs in different cities
related to the need to follow her husband in the
advancement of his career. She was a counselor/
instructor at Sante Fe Community College from 1972 to
1975. There she was honored with the Meritorious
Instructor Award. From 1975 to 1976, Mimi taught and

counseled emotionally disturbed middle school children
for the Seminole County, Florida, schools. From 1976 to
the present Mimi has been teaching psychologically
related subjects on a part-time basis for Valencia
Community College, Orlando, Florida, and Seminole Community College, Sanford, Florida, so as to be able to
devote full-time attention to her children.

I certify that I have read this study and that in my opinion it conforms to acceptable standards of scholarly presentation and is fully adequate, in scope and quality, as a dissertation for the degree of Doctor of Philosophy.

Dr. Robert O. Stripling, Chairman
Distinguished Service Professor of
Counselor Education

I certify that I have read this study and that in my opinion it conforms to acceptable standards of scholarly presentation and is fully adequate, in scope and quality, as a dissertation for the degree of Doctor of Philosophy.

Dr. Jordan B. Ray
Professor of Management

I certify that I have read this study and that in my opinion it conforms to acceptable standards of scholarly presentation and is fully adequate, in scope and quality, as a dissertation for the degree of Doctor of Philosophy.

Dr. James Wattenbarger
Professor of Educational Administration
and Supervision

I certify that I have read this study and that in my opinion it conforms to acceptable standards of scholarly presentation and is fully adequate, in scope and quality, as a dissertation for the degree of Doctor of Philosophy.

Dr. Benjamin Barger
Professor of Psychology

This dissertation was submitted to the Graduate Faculty of the Department of Counselor Education in the College of Education and to the Graduate Council, and was accepted as partial fulfillment of the requirements for the Degree of Doctor of Philosophy.

December 1979

_____
Dean, Graduate School

CPSIA information can be obtained
at www.ICGtesting.com
Printed in the USA
BVHW052121090619
550551BV00008B/284/P